A Life of a Soldier

Written By:

Justin Goose E. Shelton

Getting to Know the Author

I was born at Mission Hospital in Asheville, NC on August 5, 1988 and raised in Marshall, NC in a small community called Spillcorn. It is a very beautiful place tucked away in the mountains of Western North Carolina just a rocks throw from the Tennessee State Line. Growing up I enjoyed the outdoors, hunting, and fishing. I worked on the farm helping my uncle Robert as often as he could con me into it. About everyone in my family either cut timber or raced, most even done both. So of course I didn't want to argue with what was in my blood. I got started in dirt racing at the age of 15, and I have loved it ever since. In the community of Spillcorn there are a lot of hard working people that always tried to help one another, and that is one of my favorite things about the place. I have never seen an ugly sunrise or sunset even though we were so far back in the mountain the sun came up at 2:00 PM and set at 4:30 PM. I attending Madison High School, graduated in 2006, and went on to join the Army a year later. I always dreamed of joining, and I could just never talk myself into it. Until just like in a country song I got my heart broke by my teenage dream. It was shortly after joining the Army I went to Basic Training in February of 2008, and there I met a lot of interesting people. I started missing home a lot, and I decided to start writing down how I felt, and what I called at the time songs about what I was going through. When I returned from Training I tried to put these words I had written down into music, and to play and instrument. I learned very quickly that even though it was in my blood and a part of my heritage it was not for me. I kept writing throughout the years, I also learned to enjoy the military life. I started to think I could make a career of it. Then in 2010 I was deployed to Iraq for one year. I didn't like it so much, but while I was there I met a Soldier in the unit named Herrera. We almost instantly became best friends. She was going through a tough time, and missing home too. I shared my "songs" with her, and I discovered she wrote poetry as well. We helped each other critique one another's work. She showed me that my "songs" would work a whole lot easier as poems. That way I don't have to try to sing, and drive everyone crazy. So I started writing poems, and I really enjoyed it. Herrera died in an accident later on that year, and I didn't know what to do. It hurt me deeper than I have ever been hurt before. I really thought I was going to die of a broken heart, but with the help of friends and family I made it through. I started to enter in writing contest, and vowed to one day get a booked published. Upon returning from my deployment I thought I would never find love, but I knew I didn't want to date for the rest of my life. Before I knew it after I had given up, and lost all hope, A beautiful girl from my child hood that I would have never imagined would give me the time of day said yes to go on a date with me. Four years later the Lord blessed us with a baby boy that we named Keaton Jay Shelton. He is two now and growing faster than I want him to, but the older he gets the more I see me in him. So I guess that is ok. I guess you can say we are living in the happy ever after. Each and every day is a blessing with my family.

Table of Contents

Chapter 1: A Typical Day

It was a rainy and cool September morning in the mountains of Western North Carolina. I woke up at 0645 to the sound of the alarm going off. House of the Rising Sun by Five Finger Death Punch I thought "what a great way to start any day". I turned on the news as my middle child Emma got out of bed and wiped the sleep from her eyes to get ready for school. Emma was nine with short brown hair, green eyes, and a petite build. She was in 4th grade this year and growing faster than I could imagine. She really had a passion for horses which her bedroom reflected. Everything was horses from one wall to another.

I sat and watched the news as she got ready. The news was constantly talking about the devastation of Hurricane Harvey that had just struck Houston, Texas and now Hurricane Irma was not far behind. This one would strike Florida by Friday. Then it would be headed our way. The news bulletin read "Strongest Hurricane in History." I was getting ready for work as I listened to bits and pieces of the news. I couldn't help but hearing an update on North Korea's missile testing. North Korea had launched a few missiles to test just how far they could fire them. This had been going on a couple of months now and I think the only country that wasn't mad at them in the world was Russia. I had little time to give it much thought though it did concern me.

I had to get to work so I turned off the television and told Emma to come on, so I could take her to school. I already had the truck running and all warmed up so Emma didn't have to suffer the cold while I drove her to school. My truck was a Black 2000 Chevy Silverado that had more rust than paint, but it had good mud grips and I am pretty sure it would climb a tree if I wanted it to. We talked about her plans for the day to pass the time, even though the school was only 15 mins away.

We lived just off of Main Street in a little white double wide just outside of town, which we were renting at the time. It was just enough room for a family of five. We were about a mile outside of the city in a little college town in the mountains of North Carolina. It was in this county where my wife Renee and I had grown up and where we intended to stay until the kids were out of the house. Then we could retire and live out our remaining days in East Tennessee on some lake front property without a care in the world. That is if there is such a thing as retirement by then.

We made it to school and said our usual "bye, I love you, and hope you have a great day." Then she went in the school and I headed to work. I had to fuel up almost every other day as it seemed in the ole Chevy, but hey it got me from point A to point B. I pulled in to the fuel pump to wait my turn to fuel up.

With all of the storms moving in the coast. They decided to shut down the off shore drill rigs, so fuel prices had sky rocketed and fuel shortages were starting to spread throughout the country. As I waited my turn to get fuel. A man that was in front of me in a blue 90's model Ford Bronco was almost finished fueling and I had noticed he had glanced back at me a couple of times. It might have been because of the loud exhaust pipes on my truck which I had been meaning to get fixed, or he could have noticed my uniform. He was a bigger fella about 30 or so, he had a big beard, a long sleeve camo jacket, dark tan carhart pants, and a faded Steelers hat. I imagine he had some kind of painting job, since his clothes had paint stains of every color on them.

He hung up the nozzle and made his way back to my truck to thank me for my service and all I do for this country. This was a quiet common thing around here, it seemed to happen more often than not. I kindly thanked him for supporting what I do. He asked the usual questions like "where are you stationed?", "How many years do you have in?" and as always "Have you been across the pond?" this was a kind of a more polite way of asking if I had been deployed. I told him "I was in a Military Police National Guard unit just inside the city, which I had been in for 10 years, and that I was deployed to Iraq in 2010." We finished our conversation and I got my fuel, a couple packs of Marlboros, and headed on my way to work.

It was always a peaceful ride to work listening to classic rock and the sounds of the road as I drove. You could hear the exhaust echoing off of everything I passed and the rumble of the rough mud grip tires as I moved on out the interstate. The sun was struggling to break through the thick fog as it slowly burned off of the mountains. Most sunrises looked like a beautiful painting that should be in a gallery somewhere. I had taken many pictures of them on my phone while headed to work in the past, but this one I would have to skip. Traffic was pretty heavy this morning, and I needed both hands on the wheel.

I finally made it work with a few minutes to spare. Though normally I would make it there at least 20 mins early so I could start the coffeepot and have a smoke to get the day started off right. I went to talk to my usual crowd at the smoke pit, but do to the internet issues our usual crowd of smokers that was two or three had suddenly doubled.

I tried lighting my cigarette in the cool windy air, and had to hold my hand in a cup shape to block the wind so the lighter would burn long enough to catch the tip of tobacco on fire. It was a cooler morning than I was used to. Up until this week it had been mid 60's most mornings, but this one was around upper 40's and had a bite to it letting us know that fall was just a couple weeks away.

I took a few puffs and the Sergeant First Class (SFC) that was in charge of Soldier Readiness for the unit, SFC D as we called him. He asked me jokingly "are you ready to go to Korea or the coast for hurricane duty for a couple months?" He was in his late thirties, with hardly any hair which he kept shaved most of the time, he stood about 5'8", and had a slender build like marathon runners have.

To be honest I didn't want to go anywhere I had a 2 year old boy at home and I didn't want to leave him for a long amount of time for any reason. Jay was his name, he was a little above average height for a 2 year old. He had short blonde hair and the bluest eyes you have ever seen. He was always wide open, full of energy and very smart. To me he was the most wonderful and special gift from God I could ask for.

I didn't want SFC D to think any less of me, so I decided to give a more generic text book answer. "I guess I will go where ever y 'all want to send me". He kind of chuckled and said "good". Then he asked "Have you tried to log on your computer yet?" I simply shook my head no as I took the last puff of my cigarette and flipped the fire from the end. He said "well the internet has been down all morning. I have tried to restart the switch and router, but it still won't work". At the time this was a common thing we never really thought much of it.

I had some experience from working on computers and troubleshooting computer issues, because I had spent a lot of my down time on my deployment to Iraq hanging out with my good friend SGT Stevens. Stevens was a 6'4" red head that was skinny as a rail, and was always working out to get bigger...but it hardly happened. He was a Communications Sergeant, and he was rather good with any kind of electronics. So I tried to learn everything I could from him.

I told SFC D I would give it a look and see what I could do. I restarted the router and the switch then attempted to log on to my computer. That done the trick! It was up and working like always. A little slow but working.

I turned on the television that we had in our office to finish catching up on the latest with the storm that was moving in as I poured me a cup of coffee. It was a cheaper brand and like most military coffee it would wake the dead and gag a maggot, but it was warm and contained caffeine so I was happy. The local news was rambling on about how this storm was stronger than any other that developed in the Atlantic or that had hit the United States in history. Winds were up to 190 MPH it was described to be off of the typical category charts and guaranteed to devastate everything in its path. That kind of made me nervous, but it wasn't supposed to hit for another two days and it was headed for Florida. North Carolina was simply supposed to get five or six inches of rain depending on which region you were in the state.

This calmed my nerves a bit, but I still couldn't help but think of all of the families that would be impacted by the storm. Fortunately they had already declared a state of emergency for Florida. Which meant they had started evacuating.

The news then turned to updates on the continued flooding from Hurricane Harvey and all of its destruction. It was quiet sad to think about homes being ripped apart and everything you own being swept away in front of your eyes and all you could do is stand and watch helplessly.

At that time the phone rang. It was a deep raspy voice of an older gentlemen. It was my Battalion Sergeant Major (SGM). He said "we need to get all state active duty and Hurricane response stuff ready to go, the storm is shifting and will be hitting North Carolina Saturday morning Instead of Florida Friday." I told him "Roger, I am on it SGM." I hung up the phone and let my supervisor Master Sergeant (MSG) McDonald know what was going on.

MSG McDonald was in her early 40's, with long brown hair that she wore in a bun, and dark brown eyes. I always thought of her as my sister even though she was ten years older. She always knew what to do and always looked out for the Soldier's. Which made me respect her a lot more than most.

We made a few phone calls and got the word out of what was to come and what to expect. It would be a storm that we have never prepared for in my ten years. I took the time to do my daily routine of calling my wife and checking on her and the kids. Renee worked part time at a nursing home and was home four days a week so she could spend time with the kids and focus on what they needed. I just thank God we could afford it at the time. We talked for a while about gas prices and how the shortages were sure to come and what we needed to be prepared for the storm. I told her "go ahead and fill up your car and we will go to the grocery store when I get home."

Renee was a petite woman in her mid-30's about 5'3" with

beautiful blue eyes and a smile that could cure any sadness or anger. She had brown hair that she always kept short, and she always smelled of fruity lotions from Bath and Body Works. She was the love of my life. My one and only. We had a few problems from time to time, but nothing we couldn't work out.

It didn't seem like long after I got off the phone it was lunch time. As always my co-workers came in and gathered around to talk about work and on this day where we were on storm preparation. SFC D had his unit all notified and ready to report. He was always on top of things and usually got stuff done quicker than most. We had a mutual respect for one another, because of our similar work ethics. It wasn't long until lunch was over and it was back to work for all of us.

I started helping the other Soldier's prepare the trucks to roll out for hurricane duty. Just the basics like extra fuel cans, water jugs, and meals ready to eat (MRE's). We had got so busy taking care of trucks that we hardly noticed how fast the day went. I went and briefed MSG McDonald on our preparation completion.

Then I headed home for the day. I generally changed in to civilian clothes before heading home, so I didn't draw attention or have people questioning me. Also today I would have to stop by the High School and pick up my oldest daughter Hadley. Hadley was 14, a freshman in high school, and this year she made the Junior Varsity volleyball team. She had long brown hair that would curl like crazy if she didn't straighten it every day. She was about 5' 8" with dark brown eyes and a smile like her mothers. She had started hitting her rebellious teen years where she thought she was smarter than her mother and I, and she had mood swings that would drive any one crazy. I tried to be patient and understanding of her hormones and emotions, but it was really tough some times.

I picked her up and thank God she was in a good mood. We had our usual conversation like always. She would ask "how was your day?" I would say "good, how was yours?" This question got multiple answers depending on the day, but luckily she said "pretty good." We talked about particular events throughout our day on our way home. It was only 20 mins, but it always seemed to fly by on the "good mood" days. It was also our only just me and her time, so I really enjoyed it most days.

When we got home and I walked in the door I was greeted by my wild and overly excited little Jay bird as we called him. He was screaming "Daddy Daddy Daddy....Hold you Daddy". Which is what he always said when he wanted me to pick him up. So I did and we continued on into the living room where I was met by Renee. We kissed and asked how each other's day was as I sat down in my recliner and took off my shoes.

I ate supper and went out in the back yard to catch up on some mowing I was behind on. I worked up til dark most nights and this one was no different. It was easy to find stuff to do around the house. It seemed there was always weed eating to do or a bush needing trimmed. I got done for the day and went in to take me a shower. I generally tried to get in an hour before bed time, so I could spend time with the kids. I always made sure I told them how much I loved them every single day, because we are not guaranteed tomorrow. Well it was finally bed time, and I started to make my nightly rounds. I checked both the front and back door to make sure they were locked. I then hugged the kids and told them "good night I love you have good dreams". Then I filled Jay's sippy with water, and changed his diaper. Renee and I laid there and talked for an hour or so then said our goodnights and went to sleep. This was a typical day back then.

Chapter 2: After the Storm

Hurricane Irma ended up moving up the gulf side of Florida and headed North-West once it impacted Alabama. Tennessee got the 5 inches of rain that North Carolina was predicted to get, and basically the storm withered away into the mountains of Tennessee. North Carolina only got a couple of inches.

When I showed up to work the next morning I went to the smoke pit and to have a cigarette while the coffee pot was working its magic. No sooner than I lit my smoke SGT Frederick asked me if I caught the news. I simply said "No" and he said "After hurricane Irma moved through the Gulf of Mexico submarines were spotted in a few places at the Florida coast, and now a lot of the oil rigs in the gulf are destroyed. I think it is going to get bad man. Probably the Russians!!" This news caused a knot in my stomach. I was thinking in the back of my mind. My unit is on a 5 to 6 year rotation with deployments and this is our 6th year. Could we even fight the Russians? Could mine and Renee's relationship survive such a deployment? I said "that ain't no good man. It is cold as shit in Russia."

SGT Fredrick was my usual smoking buddy. He was my height and a fireball, like most red heads he was always mad or pissed off. We had worked together the last two years, and I don't think I have ever heard anyone cuss so much in my life. I really liked him even though he was always angry and an Eagles fan. I guess those two things go hand in hand though.

We finished our smokes and went inside to get the day started. I never turned on the news, I went to reading and answering emails instead. I worked up until lunch time and we all gathered at the table with our eyes glued to the TV. No one said a word. The news was giving an update, more oil rigs were destroyed, and more submarines had been spotted off the cost of Texas and California. Someone caught footage of one of the submarines that was blowing up the Oil Rigs. SGT Fredrick stood up and yelled "that's a Korean Submarine. Look like World War 3" The news suddenly cut to a Presidential address. It was Donald Trump behind in desk in the oval office. He gave the following speech:

"At 5:45 a.m. this morning the first wave of Korean Submarine attacks began with Oil Platform "Perdido" located in the Gulf of Mexico. The second wave started at 5:53 a.m. destroying Oil platform "Horn Mountain" just off the coast of Alabama. All remaining oil rigs and platforms in the Gulf of Mexico were ordered to evacuate immediately, but for some it was too late. The attacks ceased at 11:17 a.m. Search and rescue teams have been deployed to the Gulf. So far the death toll is 145 and hundreds injured. Almost half of the 717 Oil Platforms in the Gulf have been completely destroyed.

On December, 8 1941 President Roosevelt made the Infamy Speech after the Japanese attacked Pearl Harbor. When Roosevelt made the speech it was to inform the nation of how the attacks were carried out, and the devastation of those attacks. He also said "I ask that the Congress declare war since the unprovoked and dastardly attack by Japan on Sunday, December 7th, 1941, a state of war has existed between the United States and the Japanese Empire. (President Franklin D. Roosevelt - 1941) Well I am asking you the same today. I am asking this nation to show the world that we will not stand for this.

We as a nation will need to prepare for what is to come.

There will be many struggles as there is with every war. North Korea has set in motion an unstoppable domino effect. The next step for the United States is to declare war on North Korea, and stop this devastation. So please pray for this country and our Soldier's as we face what is ahead."

We all just sat there no one really said anything. The sound of the office phones ringing got everyone up and moving. It was Soldiers calling to see if we were deploying. Wondering what exactly was going to happen. Then MSG McDonald told me "There will be a meeting at 1500 with the Brigade commander, a lot of information was coming down, and to be ready."

Just then my cell phone rang, it was Renee she had heard the news so she was very worried, and asking questions quicker than I could answer. "Are you deploying? What am I supposed to do without you? I can't raise three kids alone." I told her "Honey please calm down, I ain't going nowhere tomorrow. If I do get deployed it will be a couple of months." I finally got her calmed down, I told her I loved her, and hung up the phone.

There wasn't a lot of information put out from the meeting, basically start getting Soldiers prepared to deploy. Also start letting your families know we will be deploying to Korea in six months. This was not good news. I don't know what I would do if I had to leave my family for a year. My last deployment it was just me...I mean sure I missed my dad, mom, and brother. This one though it was going to be a whole lot tougher on me. How could I make little Jay understand he isn't even three yet. This and many other thoughts ran through my mind.

I spent the rest of the day just thinking "how would I tell my family about something I am not even sure of?" Our last deployment to Iraq was all mortars, suicide bombers, and Improvised explosive devices (IEDs). I had always been trained for Iraq and Afghanistan, how would we train for the Korea. I went where everyone goes for answers "google". It turns out their climate is a lot like Western, NC summers average 85 degrees Fahrenheit and winters a little colder, but still around 25 degrees Fahrenheit. I always thought it was very cold and miserable there. This gave me hope. Now if I could just find a way to explain this to Renee.

Chapter 3: Breaking the News

I headed home and it seemed like I was there in just a few seconds, all of these thoughts and plans I was churning in my head. I kept saying hopefully she will understand.

When I got home I came in the door and just like always there was my little happy boy, just tickled to death to see me. I held him and gave him a kiss. I started thinking "wonder how he will take this, me being gone for a whole year or maybe forever." I had never been away from him for more than a month since he was born, and he had never spent the night away from me and his mother since he was born. My thoughts were cut short Renee walked in and said "well what did you hear." I said "let's go in the bed room to talk". We left Emma and Jay to play and watch cartoons in the living room. Hadley hadn't made it home yet. The high school bus always ran much later in the evening, so she wouldn't be home for another 20 minutes.

I sat Renee down on the bed beside me, took her hand in mine, and the words just came out. I said "honey they said we need to start preparing for a deployment in the next 12 months. Now nothing is official yet on where we may be going. We need to start making plans like, who will keep the kids while you are at work, or if you will even work at all while I am gone." Tears started to pool up in the bottom of her eye lids until they couldn't hold no more. One fell sliding slowly down her beautiful tan cheeks. I hated seeing her this way, it made me want to cry too, but I had to be strong for her and the kids. I said "Please don't cry everything is going to be fine. It is just a year and I will be back. Plus we could use the extra money." She got a little angry at this "we don't need the money. I need you here with me and the kids....you can get a job at ingles for all I care. We can sell stuff so you don't have to go" she said. I said "let's talk more about it later. Hadley will be home soon and we need to tell the kids." Still with a little anger in her voice she said "we will tell them tonight before bed." I said "fine, but I want to go tell my dad and my brother face to face, just like I had done on my first deployment." She agreed.

Hadley got home a few minutes later and we all loaded up in the truck to go over to my dad's place. It was 45 minutes away, but luckily it was church night, so my brother will hopefully be over there since he is a preacher at the church my dad goes to. I thought hey I can get both of them together at once. They already been through this before so this should be easier for them.

We got to my dad's about an hour before dad had to leave for church, and just like planned my brother was there too. I tried to make small talk and get them away from the crowd so I said "Dad are you still working on that 67 in the garage." He said "yeah. Want to see it?" "I said "sure." We all hadn't been in the garage together since I gave up dirt track racing when Jay was born. So I am sure they figured something was up.

When I stepped into the garage I had to squeeze in to get past the big blue tarp dad draped over this ole truck. Dad flipped the lights on and slid the tarp back. It was a flat black long wheel base 1967 Chevy C-10. It had the big chrome hub caps, and skinny orange pin stripe running the length of the truck. She looked a whole lot better than the day dad rolled it off the trailer.

I said "she looks good." Dad said "you ain't asked about this truck in two years and that was when you told me Renee was pregnant, with Jay so what is going on?" I said "well it's not a baby this time." Trying to break the tension. I said "my unit has been put on standby to deploy. We have six months to prepare." Dad said "figures…I told you to quit signing that dotted line." I said "that dotted line is what keeps my family fed." He said "well you done alright last time I am sure you will be fine." I simply agreed yes, I didn't want to say I'm nervous, I'm older, and I have a family now. My brother said "we will be praying for you like always'". I said "thanks, but what I really need is for you two to help Renee. This is the first time for her, and you two are used to it." My brother said "ha-ha used to it? You never get used to that. You just wait for a phone call someone saying he has been hurt, or killed, or for you to call and say I am coming home."

On my last deployment I had been in a small accident that resulted in my appendix rupturing. My father got a phone call from some man in the Military. He said "your son has been in an accident, he is in surgery and we will call you when he wakes up." I woke up and called my father to let him know everything was ok, and he was so happy to hear my voice. He said "they called me two days ago and wouldn't tell me anything."

My dad was 56 years old with more grey than red hair now. He had blue eyes and always wore a close cut beard. My last deployment really seemed to take a toll on him. He used to tell me he aged ten years while I was gone. I really think he did. His hair had turned almost completely grey, and he had more wrinkles when I got home. A deployment is not easy on anyone in the military or their family members. Everyone is affected differently, but all has their troubles and worries when it comes to deploying to a combat zone.

My dad said "I am glad your grandfather isn't here to hear his grandson is headed to the same place he was 70 years ago." My grandfather fought in the Korean War. He was a tank driver through multiple deployments over there. He never would talk about it at all. I am sure he seen things only nightmares are made of. He was the only other person in my family that served, so when I signed up no one was really thrilled to hear the news. I said "yeah I am sure he would be a little mad."

We stood and talked a while longer and then it was time for my dad and brother to head to church. My brother had to be there a little early to turn on the lights and the heat. I guess that was normal stuff the preacher done. He said "we are headed to church if you want to come." He said stuff like that every once and a while. He never really pushed the issue though like a lot of other church members I knew, and I really respected him a lot more for it. I said "I might one day."

My brother was two years older than me, about 3 inches shorter, and every bit of 80lbs lighter. Mom always said "I took all the food and milk when we were little." ha-ha. He had dark brown hair and usual kept a goatee or a thin beard. He was definitely the better brother of us both. He was a preacher man and family man long before I ever got started. He straightened right up after high school, found God and started a Family. I was always the drinking and partying one.

It took me til after my deployment to meet Renee and calm down. I mean I still like to have a few beers on the weekend, but it was much different now. I can truly say she saved me from my demons. I had come back from Iraq in a mess. I was drinking everyday doing anything to go to sleep. I was numb in a lot of ways and I kind of wanted to be. She showed me how to let go of the past and to live for the present. Sure I still had the occasional nightmare but nothing like back then. I thanked God every day for her.

We loaded up and headed home. It was a quiet drive all the way home just some country music playing on the radio and the roar of the Chevy. As we crossed the mountain headed home you could see all of the colors of fall as the leaves were turning orange, red, and almost yellow. It was a clear sign that summer was gone, and it was almost time to start collecting firewood. We don't have a wood stove, but my dad, uncle, two cousins, and I would get together every year around this time to cut wood for my grandmother, two aunts, and my uncle. It was hard work but someone had to do it.

We got home around 7:30 p.m. which was almost dark at that time of year. I told the girls to get their baths took and get ready for school the next day. Once they were done we sat them down on the couch together. This is how we would always break news of a loved one passing, or of some major change coming soon in their life. Both of them seemed pretty nervous.

I started by saying "girls I have been slotted to deploy to Korea within the next year. I want to make this year the best one yet, and I do not want you two to worry everything will be ok." They said "ok" with a sound of sadness in their voices. I said "do you have any questions for me." Hadley still with a nervous confused look on her face shook her head no. She was a lot like her mom she never really showed a lot of emotion. She was more of a "don't let people see me worry or cry type". Emma of course had questions "what will we do while you are gone?" She was always the more curious type. It took longer to get the point across to her but she was very smart. I said "you will go to school and help your mama every chance you get. She will need help with your brother and around the house." She said "ok, but who will take us out on the boat at the lake, and fish with us at the kids fishing tournament?" I said "you can still go to the pool, and mom can help with the fishing. Try not to worry about stuff honey." We said our good nights and I love you, then headed to bed.

It was a quieter night than expected. Renee didn't ask any questions. She just said" I love you so much Mister, you mean the world to me and I don't know if I can make it without you." I said "I love you much more and you are my everything." We said stuff like this all the time, but this night it seemed to mean a whole lot more. I said "everything is going to be ok. I know units that have been sitting on the plane ready to leave, and got the whole deployment called off." She said "ok I just worry about you crazy!"

Chapter 4: Planning for the Year

One of the most difficult things about getting ready to deploying is picking up and leave everything for one year. There are some simple questions like who will cut my lawn? On my first deployment I just crammed everything in a storage shed, I didn't leave anyone power of attorney, I signed the title to my truck and left it with my dad, and I am pretty sure I had the shortest will in history. It read "full military honors and I want Uncle Jessie to walk behind the casket. Give my brother all my possession's." Pretty lame I know, but I was 19 years old. How many 19 year olds can sit down and write out their will? Plan than funeral or who gets what? The truth about it was I didn't own a lot at the time. Just a pickup truck and I mainly rented everywhere I had lived.

Not only do you have to worry about simple personnel possessions you have to account for who will do these things while I am gone. Who will cut firewood for my mother in-law? I guess I can order some. Who will put Emma on the bus at 7:15 a.m. in the morning when Renee has to be at work by 6:00 a.m.? It can become over whelming and quite stressful if you let it. Yes, Renee and I had been together for some years now, but we did not have joint bank accounts, car insurance, or even telephone bills. I need to take my kids on a special trip. Something more memorable than usual. We hadn't been to the beach as a family in years! You try not to get hung up on the what ifs, but it is good to have a backup plan just in case. I mean who wants to leave a struggle or burden behind for your family to deal with.

Renee and I sat down one night and laid out a plan for what bills need to be joint, what bills we should pay off with the extra money from the deployment, and what things we needed to do to make this next year the best for the kids. Even though I hate pictures we both agreed to take pictures of everything.

One nice thing about the military is it has family programs that will help the spouse with common issues they will encounter while you are deployed. There is a couple of yellow ribbon ceremonies to explain stuff to your family before you leave and after you return to make the process much easier.

There was a few things I knew I had to do. I had to write my letters to each family member. When a Soldier deploys they write their letter or letters for their family members to read in the event something happens to them and they don't come home from the deployment. I wanted my family to know how I felt and how much they meant to me. Other than saying I love you I was never quite the romantic type, and to be honest I don't think Renee was either.

One night it was our third or fourth anniversary. I lit candles and put them all through the house, then I put fake rose pedals all in the floor leading to the bath tub. I called her to see when she would be home. No kids tonight I thought. When she was close I ran a nice hot bath. I put some of those bath balls in there to make the water all pretty. I sat her favorite drink (Mountain Dew) on the side of the tub. Everything was so perfect and ready for her to come home. I went and sat in the living room with just the T.V. on otherwise the whole house was dark. She came in the door….said "what the?" she walked straight to me in the living room, and said "what are you trying to say I need a bath?" I said "I was trying to be romantic gosh!" So after that I gave up on sweet stuff other than sending some flowers on Valentine's Day, and the occasional date night.

I decided I would need to write my dad, brother, Renee,

and all three kids would get one each. I also wanted to do a father daughter/son day with each kid. Just the two of us doing whatever they wanted to do. I figure I could do somethings to be a better dad over the next year. I had been spending a lot of time mowing the yard and clearing brush and just not spending the time with my family they deserve.

Chapter 5: Training Begins

In the National Guard you usually get one year to train up for the deployment, then go to a mobilization site for a month or two, then fly to your deployment country. That means we would start planning for a country that no U.S. Soldier had fought in, in 70 years. I took the time to do some of my own research. I felt as me being the Battalion Training NCO I should try to get all of the knowledge I could on our new found enemy. The first thing I learned was that there were 54,246 American Soldier's killed in the Korean War. We were preparing to send 100,000 and I would hope the casualties never got anywhere close to that number. It would be a scary one that is for sure with all of the missiles and nuclear bombs.

I had to find a way to start preparing my Soldier's. We would get a three week annual training this year leading up to the deployment. So realistically other than the training we would receive at the mobilization site we would have 45 actual training days (going off of the 1 weekend a month 3 weeks this year) to prepare. I said "that's not enough time." But how much time is enough? On my last deployment I seen a few guys that were really high speed leading up to the deployment, and I said "there is a guy to look to when shit gets bad." I am afraid I couldn't of been more wrong. A Solider will amaze you when the bullets go to flying and the mortars or missiles start exploding a few yards away. That is simply nothing you prepare yourself for.

As Military Police our mission would be to simply guard the main base, control entry and exiting of the base, or be clearing buildings in hot zones or danger zones. This I was not a fan of, we had ran many training scenarios of clearing rooms or buildings and every time the instructor would point out someone that would get shot or be killed. Small things we missed or skipped over when searching, but the only way to learn is through trial and error and Train! Train! Train!

Why couldn't this mission be like the one in Iraq, and we could all be prison guards? Not outside the wire where the bad stuff happens. Where you come back with bits and pieces of your friends, and a lifetime of nightmare that haunt you.

Either way no matter the situation my team was going to be ready for anything. I had two Soldiers that were assigned to me, neither of which had been deployed. One was 19 his name was Swann he had been in the military for 3 years and the closest thing he came to a deployment was playing call of duty for hours on a Saturday night. Swann had been married for a month or so. He was the one I would later look his wife in the face and promise her he would come home safely. This is something we say to make family members feel better, but it was no guarantee. Swann had longer blonde hair on top and a close cut on the side. He kept me in trouble with the squad leader because his hair barely was in regulation. I had to measure it every drill. It drove me crazy. He was a sharp Soldier that attended college part time, and always passed the Army Physical Fitness Test (APFT) no problem. He was studying to get his bachelor's degree in criminal justice.

My other Soldier was an overweight 26 year old that still lived with his parents, and the rumor was he liked to drink a little too much and get rowdy. His name was Perkins. Perkins was six feet and 230lbs. yes, the Army says that is overweight. He had brown hair that he always kept in a very short high and tight. He had tattoos that covered his arm, he said each one told a story. One was a band aid on his wrist that he once explained to me. It was to remind him of his struggle with addiction in his younger years. It is almost unheard of to be in the Army 8 years without a deployment, but sometimes it happens.

When preparing for a deployment in my opinion range day is one of the most important days. This is the day we get to see who can shoot and who can't. I always took pride in helping struggling shooters and teaching them how to correct their mistakes. Perkins amazed me by shooting a 36 out of 40 he only missed two of the 300 meter targets and 2 of the 250 meter targets. That is pretty impressive I think.

Swann didn't do so well. He failed to qualify the first time. So he came over to me and told me he didn't qualify and asked me to go up with him next time and coach him. I agreed to do so without hesitation. I said "first let's step over here of to the side and see what you are doing wrong." This is what we call primary marksmanship instruction or PMI. The Soldier holds the weapon in the prone position (lying down on their stomach). Then they focus on a fixed target and go through the motions of what they do while firing the weapon.

We teach there are four things that are needed to fire a weapon successfully. (1) Weapon grip (how you hold the weapon). (2) Sight picture (make sure you have a clear view through the pep sight or rear sight post going down to the front sight post). (3) Breath control. (4) Trigger squeeze. Take a deep breath and breathe out on the natural pause squeeze the trigger until the weapon discharges then repeat. Do not jerk or pull the trigger and you should be fine.

Well Swann had never fired a weapon except in basic training, so he was doing the most common error. He was squeezing the grip like it was a shotgun and was going to jump out of his hands at any second. I spotted it immediately, because around the edges of his palms were white where he was squeezing so tight. I gave him a couple pointers and we stepped back up to the firing line. He shot a 24 out of 40. This was barely passing, so I told him we would work on it some more before the deployment.

The next main training event was the pepper spray and Taser certification. All military policeman have to be certified to carry pepper spray and a Taser. Sadly there is only one way to get certified. You have to ride the lightning (get tased) and feel the burn (get pepper sprayed in the eyes and face). Perkins and I had already completed this task when we were preparing for state active duty on the North Carolina Reaction Force back in 2007. Basically we were deployed inside the state if there was a large riot or if a protest got out of hand.

Poor ole Swann though I am afraid he would have to do it. He seemed a bit worried, so I tried to keep him calm by giving him a few tips. Like after they spray you shake all of the excess from you face. This will keep it from running down on your neck or chest. Also after you complete the pepper spray obstacle course, rinse your face, then put baby shampoo all over it, and stay away from those fans it will reactivate when you walk away from them. He took the pepper spray about as well as anyone else. He didn't scream or cuss like some of the others. He kept his composure and got through the course just fine and even took my advice. "Not too bad I thought." It made me feel better as a leader to know that when he was in a world of pain he still listened to me.

Next was the Taser, and I am not going to lie it hurts. I

remember when I got tased it felt like every bone in my body was being squeezed to the brink of exploding. Swann took it like a champ he didn't scream like a girl, he didn't cuss like a sailor, he just gritted and took it. This really impressed me. When it was done he got up and came over to me. I said "well?" He said "that was rough." I said "you done well though." I think it is good to try to build a Soldiers confidence with compliments on a Job well done.

Chapter 6: The Last Few Months

We were down to the last few months before we deploy. I was really impressed at how well my two Soldier's performed during training and preparation leading up to this point. Perkins had lost a few pounds, and was in the best shape of his life. Swann had learned quite a bit.

Now it was time to take care of the family and focus on their wants and needs. Basically spoil the crap out of them, and give them some happy thoughts to think about when they are missing me. I know it isn't text book, but it is how I was going to do it.

I started with a one week trip to Charleston, South Carolina. It truly is such a beautiful place and nowhere near as crowded as Florida. I would do everything I could to stay away from them Florida drivers anyways. It was a nice drive all the way there as we left the mountains and traveled through the heart of South Carolina. "What a beautiful state I thought" as I drove down the highway, passing farms, and small towns.

We stayed in a hotel at Folly beach. It was a little higher than most, but can you really put a price on the best memories my family would have of me if this deployment went wrong? I will never forget when we got close enough to smell the ocean the kids were so excited. Hadley was telling Jay and Emma stories from when she was a kid going to the beach. The last time Emma was there she was real little so she didn't remember and Jay has never been. So this was going to be a great trip.

We literally done everything the kids wanted to do. We hit waterparks we practically lived on the beach. It was so perfect just watching the kids in the water. Jay would chase the water back out and run away when a wave was crashing in. Hadley and Emma made some pretty cool sand art just in time for Jay to come running through and destroy it.

In the evenings we would eat supper the lay by the pool as the kids played and jumped around in the water having the time of their lives. The sun would slowly fade from the sky as it dove into the sea making the most beautiful colors I have ever seen in a sky. Then darkness would slowly close in as the stars grew brighter. Every second was truly magical.

Before we knew it we were loaded up and headed back to the beautiful mountains of Western North Carolina. I would have to admit it was one of the best family vacations we had ever had. The kids had a really good time too. On the way home we told stories and talked about the things we done that week. It really made the five hour drive fly by.

Next I wanted to take Renee on a date that was better than any other we had been on. We had always went somewhere nice to eat for our anniversary, but this was going to be different. We started off the evening going to the nicest Steak house in the city. Their steak was so soft and mouthwatering. The waitress treated us like royalty which we wasn't quite used to since we usually didn't go anywhere nicer than the diner in town. Then we went to the local spa for a 30 minute massage followed by a one hour soak in the hot tubs. It was so relaxing all of my worries and stress were drowned out by the flow of the hot water on my back. While we were in the hot tub I could tell something was wrong. I said "what's a matter honey?" Renee said "this day is so perfect. What if this is our last date together?" I said "let's not be worrying about stuff like that." She said "it is all I can think about as time gets closer." I said "everything is going to be fine you will see. We are going to grow old together at the lake." She said "I hope you are right." I said "I usually am." And smiled. This made her smile. We ended the night at the bakery in town where they serve the best carrot cake in the world. Just enough icing to cake ratio…it will almost bring a tear to your eye.

Hadley was the one I figured would be the hardest, so I took her out for her day next. We went and watched some love story were of course the main character dies in the end. After it was over she was crying and If I'm being honest I had to fight some tears back myself. I asked "why do you like to watch that sad stuff?" She said "I don't know I just do." I said "ok then." She asked "you're not going to die over there are you?" I said "no, me and your mom have our own love story to live." Trying to make her laugh, but as usual she didn't. I said "I have to be here to run off the man you want to marry kiddo, so I'm not going anywhere." This made her smile. In the back of my mind I thought I hope I don't let my family down. I love them so much and I just have to come home to them they need me.

Finally the day came where it was Emma's turn. She was so excited, she had all kinds of plans, most of all she wanted to ride horses. I gave in and took her to a local trail ride place. Basically you pay money to rent horses for a couple of hours and ride trails with a guide. I grew up riding horses so I didn't mind. Emma had only rode a couple of horses that someone would lead. She climbed up on top of the horse with a little help of course. I lead her around a minute, and then I said "Do you think you can handle him?" By him I meant a 12 year old black quarter horse. Poor ole thing should have been retired in an open field somewhere. She said "I guess." It turns out she was a natural. I was very proud of the way she handed the horse. You would think she had been riding for years.

While we were riding she had to ask a few questions that she had been thinking about. She said "How will you talk to us while you are over there?" I said "well I am sure they have phones and if they don't I can message y 'all on the internet, or write a letter." She said "good, because I will have to tell you what I done at school and how my day was." I said "yes, you will." This kind of made me sad and realize how much I was going to miss that little devil. I didn't have much time to think about it until the next question came. She asked "can I write you letters and draw you pictures while you are gone." I said "of course, and I hope you do. That will make me very happy." She smiled her biggest smile. Then she asked another "when you get back can we do this again." I love this, I really hope I can get my own horse one day." I said "I am sure you will have your own horses one day." It was all the kid thought about.

After we got done with the trail ride we went to the local ice cream shop. Emma got Orange sherbet in a waffle cone which was her favorite. I got a strawberry cheesecake shake which was amazing. Then it was on to the go cart track and arcade. We rode go carts for an hour and spent forty dollars in coins in a matter of minutes it seemed. Then like always stood there waiting on her to spend 500 tickets that I begged her to just give to some little kid. She got what she wanted and they put her couple of items in a bag for her.

We got to the car and I asked "well what did ya get?" She held up a spider ring and a little spinning top. I said "is that it?"

She said "no I got you some cards." I asked "what do you mean cards?" She said "playing cards to play when you are bored." I said "well thank you." Emma was always the most generous when it came to buying people stuff. She had a good heart, one of the most kind nine years olds I have ever met. She opened the pack to look at them and she pulled out the joker. She said "it looks like you, maybe it can be your good luck charm." I said "Yeah I could always use some luck". She said "maybe it will keep you safe." I said "thank you so much. I love you Emma." The card was out of some knock off deck just a weird blue pattern on the back. The joker was black and white with a fan in one hand and pointing with the other. He looked a little silly with his big jester hat, and his long stockings hanging off the bottom of his feet. I guess you can say he looked like me. Ha-ha

Jay was a bit harder since he was two and if you asked what he wanted to do. He would say "Cartoons or Thomas (the train)." So that is what we did we went to a day out with Thomas on the Tweetsie railroad. It was a two hour drive, but so worth it when I saw his face light up and start screaming Thomas! Thomas! Thomas! They had a little country fair set up, a petting zoo, and he actually got to ride Thomas the train. He was the happiest little guy in the world that day. We played and I just followed him around until dark. Looking at whatever and doing whatever he wanted. He fell asleep no more than a mile or two down the road on the way home. I felt real good about myself, just thinking about what I had done with my kids in the last few months and how much fun we had. I wish it would all never end. I whispered a little prayer "thank you lord for blessing me with this great family and these wonderful kids. Please help them through the tough times they face over the next year or so Amen."

Chapter 7: Almost time

The deployment was just 3 weeks away now. Renee and I was running down the final checklist. We got a joint bank account, gave my Military orders to deploy to the cell phone company my phone would shut off the day after I leave. We went and got her car insurance added to mine, and set up a couple of automatic withdraws on monthly bills, like lights, water, and the car payment. My best friend Bill lived just a mile or two away so he agreed to mow my yard and weed eat.

Bill was about my father's age, he had salt and pepper hair with a mustache. Bill and I talked almost every day for at least 15 minutes or so. We talked about everything, how our day was, what we planned to do that evening, and what we got done over the weekend. We were neighbors down in the little campground by the lake, so we saw each other almost every weekend in the summer. Then in the winter months we would get together and play cards way up in the night. He was just like a brother or uncle to me. We were close friends and he meant a lot to me. I listened to every word he ever told me.

I had told Bill if something ever happened I would want him to be the one to tell Renee. He said "Now don't be talking like that." I said "just promise me." and he did.

My dad, uncle, and brother pitched in and we were able to cut my mother in-law enough firewood to last her two winters. Yeah, everything was really coming together. I took out a personal loan to pay off the credit card and the other small loan we had for the golf cart we had bought a few years back, and I had just enough left over to put new tires on Renee's Toyota Rav 4. I mean it is not like I could run home and change a flat.

My brother just lived about six miles away, so he agreed to

come by or at least call to check on Renee and the kids every so often. He was really a big help in getting the place cleaned up the way I wanted it before I left. Since I would be leaving in June we piled and burned brush, trimmed all the trees and bushes, cleaned out the shed, and organized most of my Military gear.

He was a good brother, and a great father. We were never the loving hugging type of family, but he knew I loved him. I always gave him a hard time about needed to work harder and not take so many naps.

I really tried to help people all the time this was a real passion of mine. If I was by myself I would often stop and help stranded motorist, or maybe someone that lost a few bales of hay off a trailer. My brother helped people too, but his was more of a spiritual help. He was a good man, I could only hope my son was like him one day.

Renee and I decided to take a Saturday and go over to visit my dad. It always made me feel good driving over to his house. The true feeling of going home, all of the familiar sites, and the memories that came rushing back. We got there and spent most of the day just sitting and watching T.V. and talking about NASCAR, fishing, and hunting. This was usual conversation at dad's house. We played outside with the kids, and as always Jay ended up in the creek. He came to me soaking wet, and asked "what happened?" I said "you got in the creek didn't you?" He said "yes, Help me" as he was tugging trying to get his wet shirt that was sticking to him off.

Dad let out a big laugh he said "he is just like you" Renee quickly agreed. I just shot her a look and stuck my tongue out at her, which made her smile. I helped dad drag out the grill and we grilled a few hamburgers. I was trying to show him how to be a grill master and he was trying to tell me I didn't know what I was doing. Either way the burgers turned out great.

We ate and before long it was time to leave and head home. We got in the car and said our good byes then rolled on home. I couldn't help but think of what a lucky man I was to have such and awesome brother and caring father.

The next day we decided we would drive out to Tennessee, visit my mother, and pull the boat home. Since I wouldn't be around to drive it. My mom lived in East Tennessee she was in her late fifty's and she was plum grey headed. I hadn't seen her in a while because she lived so far away. Sure we talked on the phone every once and a while, but nothing like her and my brother did. I hate to admit it, but I broke the news to her over the phone when we found out about the deployment. She was a typical country woman that spent most her of her time in the garden and working around home. She never really went many places.

We wasn't that close, and hadn't been since papaw died (her father). His name was Gene and he was my hero. I looked up to him since I was a little bitty fella. When he died it about killed me. I didn't even attend the funeral, which often regretted.

I hugged her and gave her a kiss on the forehead. She seemed to age a lot since the last time I seen her....come to think of it I can't remember when it was, Christmas I guess. I could've made more of an effort to talk to her, but I was a little stubborn and always said "the phone works both ways if she wants to talk she can call me." She played with the grand-kids a while and then it was time to go. I wanted to get to the lake and load the boat before dark. I told her I loved her and we left. We made it to the lake about an hour before dark, and I got the boat loaded just in time to see one of the most beautiful sunsets melting into the trees on the far side of the lake. That is why I loved this place so much. Everything about it was so wonderful. I was going to miss this place.

Chapter 8: Shipping Out

The day finally come to pack up and ship out. It is funny how when you are dreading something like when you have to leave time fly's, but the day you look forward to like coming home seems to take forever. We rode to the event together no one said a whole lot, so I took the time to say a lot of my good byes. That way we didn't have that crying emotional good bye, and I would be able to talk without fighting tears. I said "it won't be long and I will be home. I love all of you very much. I will call and write everyday so y'all don't have to worry about me. Before you know it you will be driving to the airport to pick me up to come home. I need all of you to stick together and help your mom." They all in a real sad voice said "ok".

The deployment ceremony was like most. We marched in, the band played a few songs, a congressman would make a speech, the Chaplin would say a prayer for our protection, a few ranking individuals would make their speeches, and we would stand up and march out.

Then was the hardest part saying good bye to our families before we got on the bus and was escorted by the local Police all the way to the airport.

I hugged all of them and told them each something just for them. I started with little man. He was confused why his sister's and mom was crying. I knelt down and he said "why mama cry?" why sissy cry?" I was fighting the tears pretty hard by this time. I said "daddy has got to go on a trip with his friends. Ok?" I said "you are the big man in the house now." He said "hold you" I picked him up and said "will you take care of mommy while daddy is gone?" He said "yes" with a confused look on his face. I handed him to Renee and said "be a good boy." He said "ok"

Now I had to try to clear my throat to talk to Emma. I leant down kissed her forehead and put my hand on her shoulder I said "I am going to be back and we will ride horses again baby" she said "ok, I will miss you bunches." She said "do you have the card for luck?" I pulled it from my breast pocket on my uniform and showed her." She said "I'm not worried then." I said "that's a good girl. I am proud of you for being strong honey. You be good for your mama."

Then I slid on down the line to Hadley. There was no leaning or kneeling. She had grown so big she was my height almost. My little girl would be driving in another year, and she was so beautiful like her mother. She already had a stream of tears headed down each cheek. I leaned in and said "it's ok to let people see you cry that's how they know you care about them." She said "I am scared" I tried to speak, but I had to clear my voice, my throat was burning trying to fight back the tears. No matter how hard I tried I couldn't stop them. My cheeks had tears running down them and I didn't care. Just like the day she was born, and I became a father. I cleared my throat, and said "you have to be mama's helper now". She said "I will" I said just think one volleyball season, and soccer season then I will be home. You know how fast they go by. Then when I get home we can talk about a car." She kind of smiled. By this time her cheeks were soaked.

Then last was Renee my one true love. The woman that made me a father, a husband, and a true family man. I wish I had prepared something better to say to her by this time there was little wet spots on her shirt where she had been crying. She was holding Jay and he still didn't know what was happening. I just wanted to remember that moment forever she looked so beautiful. She had her hair fixed nice. She eye liner out lined her beautiful blue eyes and made them pop like I had never noticed before. I just kind of stared. She said "give me a kiss" I did and she said "you better come home to me. I don't need a hero I need you home". I said "I will do my best." She said "you better." I think she knew I needed that firmness at this point. I kissed her and said "take care of the kiddos and keep this little man straight. I kissed him one last time and gave them all a prolonged hug. Then I turned and grabbed my bags. Jay started hollering "Daddy! Daddy! Daddy! Like he had done out of excitement when I came home from work so many times before. This time was different he was crying and it was killing me. I didn't look back I couldn't I would lose it, and my family didn't need to see that right now.

I slid my bags in the compartment in the bottom of the charter bus and walked up on the bus. I made my way to my seat and sat down. I looked out the window at my family all of them crying just standing there watching this big bus roll away with me in it. Renee was rocking back and forth trying to calm Jay, but nothing would work except his daddy and I couldn't be there. I wish I could, but I had a job to do. I laid my head in my lap and just let loose. I cried like I had never cried before.

When we got to the airport we unloaded the bus and loaded everything on the airplane that we would be flying to Ft. Bliss, TX for our final training before we flew out. I don't remember a lot about the plane ride because I was so sad and really missed my family. I tried to hide how I was feeling from my Soldier's, but they felt the same way I am sure.

The next few weeks at FT Bliss, TX flew by. It was just a

bunch of waiting in line, getting shots, going to classes, and checking the box on required training. We ran the Prison in the huge training area they had just like my last deployment training to go into Iraq.

We still wasn't sure what our mission would be when we hit the ground in Korea. I called Renee and the kids every chance I got. She seemed to be fine for now since I was still in the states. Everything seemed to be going ok at home. Luckily we had an app on our phones we could video chat with, so I got to see the kid's every day. I bought a laptop so I could continue to video chat if there was internet where we were going.

We got 2 days of leave before we reported back to fly out for the deployment. A lot of people went home, but I couldn't put myself through that again. I guess you could say I was selfish, but I just couldn't do it. I stayed around El Paso, TX with some friends I had made so far.

One of the friends name was Cody Southern. He was a big weight lifter that had black hair, stood about 6 feet, and had arms the size of my legs. He was a little cocky like most weight lifters, but he was a good ole country boy like myself maybe that's why we got along so well. He was also a Sergeant that had been in the Army 10 years, so we could talk about stuff like how it was before the Army got sensitive and softer. He had never been deployed, though he did have a lot of knowledge about Military Police (MP) Operations. I was happy he was the other team leader in the squad with me. He was also born and raised in Texas, so he knew how we could kill some time and keep our mind off of home.

We hit the horse track which is something I had never done before. I thought it was pretty cool watching the horses race, and the gamblers reaction to how their horse done. Some people really got a little too in to it. They were yelling to coach their horse they had bet on up until it would lose. Then they were yelling, cussing, and ripping up tickets. It was quite amusing to watch.

Next we went and checked in to a little hotel that I couldn't pronounce. We were pretty hungry so we went next door to a bar and grill. The food was amazing, I had a couple of beers and then we turned in for the night. When I laid down I couldn't get Renee and the kids off of my mind. So I tossed and turned most of the night, just thinking of them and wondering what they were doing. I finally fell asleep around one or two in the morning.

The next morning I woke up around 8 am and went down to get me a cup coffee at the hotels complimentary breakfast. The breakfast ended up being a choice of cereal, muffins, or donuts that looked a month old. I just got my coffee and made my way outside to have a smoke. I found a concrete barrier at the edge of the parking lot to sit on while I drank my coffee. It was a warm Saturday morning in Texas, and my last day in the states. I just sat there and watched cars driving by on the busy two lane road in front of the hotel. I got to thinking "wonder where they are headed? I am sure some are going to work, others had kids in the car, so maybe a family trip."

It really got me to missing home, so I called Renee. She answered and I asked "can I call you on video." She said "yeah" so we hung up and I called her back on Video chat. I said "good morning baby cakes." That was her nickname I had gave her not long after we said I love you for the first time. She said "good morning". She was still in bed even though they were 2 hours ahead of us, which meant it was 11 there. She still had the just woke up voice with a bit of what I call the bed head. Still beautiful as ever though. It reminded me of all of the mornings I would wake up before her and watch her sleep a few seconds, before I got up and got the day started. I asked "how is everyone?" She said "good". I said "I love and miss all of you very much." She said "we love and miss you too." She turned the camera where I could see little Jay sleeping. She said "your baby boy is going to sleep all day." I said "that is ok. Look at how beautiful that boy is. I wish I could be there to hold him." She said "you will before long." I said "yep. We fly out in the morning, and we will be stopping in Kuwait so I don't know when I can call." She said "ok, you will call tonight though won't you?" I said "of course I wouldn't be able to sleep if I didn't." She said "ok I will talk to you then." We said our I love you's and hung up. We never did really talk on the phone long when I was on the road, mainly because the conversation would turn sad.

      I went back up to the room and asked Southern "what are we doing today?" we have to report back by 1700. He said "whatever you want to do, but let me call the wife first." He had been married for 2 years and they didn't have any children yet, but I think they were trying before he had to leave. I said "yeah you better. I just got off the phone with Renee." He called his wife while I took a shower. Once I came out he asked "are you ready to go." I said "is everything ok at home". He said "yep, she is just worried." I said "yeah Renee is too, but what can we do?" He said "just suck it up and deal with it I guess". He never really showed any emotion. He was like the old school leaders I had when I was a private. He had to be hard and tough I guess.

      We went and wasted away the day just driving around, got

a bite to eat and reported back 30 minutes early. We had an accountability formation at 1715, and then it was time to pack up everything we wasn't sleeping in ,or on that night and get ready to roll first thing the next morning.

The next morning started early. We had formation went over instructions of how the flight and day was going to go, and then loaded in the airplane. It was a civilian commercial plane that would be carrying us to Kuwait and making one stop in Ireland to fuel up. 18 hours on an airplane what a joy! I slept most of the time, and if you have never been on a flight that long. The flight personnel tells you to untie and loosen you shoes, so it don't cause blood clots that could kill you. I thought that would be a horrible way to go. Die before you even start the deployment.

We made it to Kuwait the next day or at least I think. I still had my watch set to home time, Texas was 2 hours behind home, and Kuwait was 7 hours head so it was confusing at first.

Chapter 9: We made it to Kuwait

We got off the plane and got our housing assignments, we were not even sure how long we would be staying. On my last deployment when I was headed to Iraq we stayed in Kuwait for 1 week to get acclimated to the heat, and let our bodies adjust. This time we were headed for colder country so I am not sure what were even doing there. We did have good internet though so I was very happy about that. I would video chat with Renee as soon as I got settled in.

I didn't even have time to unpack my duffle when my Platoon Sergeant called us over for a meeting. His name was SFC Gary Booker, he was another old school SGT that didn't take shit from no one and he told you how it was, and you better fix it or he would fix you. He was my height and very skinny with grey hair, and a small grey mustache. I respected more than most, and to be honest I was quite scared of him. He was not a big man, but when he got mad and yelled you better listen.

We went in a tent where other platoons were for the meeting. SFC Booker spoke up and said "alright listen up." The room instantly went quiet. He said "North Korea tested a Rocket yesterday that is capable of reaching the United States. The president has ordered a series of bombings for the next week. We are anticipating North Korea to bomb South Korea as well. As soon as the bombing ends we are heading in. There is already a Theatre Interment Facility (TIF) next to the border of North and South Korea we will be taking over. It is small and barely operation. We will be giving it some upgrades and making it a bit more functional to our needs. Infantry will be the first wave in to North Korea after the Bombings. They will simply be doing a quick sweep. Any captives will be collected and brought to us to hold until further notice. We will also have a…

collection team searching and clearing buildings for any threats just north of the boarder. We have the right to search any building or property. There is expected to be over thousands of casualties in South Korea. All military family members have already been evacuated. Get your men ready this is the real deal, so don't screw this up."

I went back and briefed my team on the information that was passed down. I wanted them to be ready and to be prepared. I dismissed them and they went back to their tents. Our tents were big tan ones that actually had a nice air conditioning and lights inside. A drash tent as the Army called it. I unpacked my bags and decided to take a shower.

We had shower trailers that had 4 individual stalls, so I hurried to get ahead of the crowd. The shower trailers were pretty nice, Even though the water never really got hot. You really didn't need hot water when it was 80 degrees at night. I took my shower and got into my sleeping clothes. We slept in our Army physical training uniforms. Which was the grey Army t-shirts with black army shorts, which was quite comfortable I thought. It was much better than the white sweat pants and sweater marshmallow uniform we slept in during basic training.

I decided I would call Renee and check in. I pulled up my laptop and purchased 24 hours of Wi-Fi for the wonderful price of $4.99. I figured I would just buy it day by day and see how long we would be here. I called and sure enough she answered. Now the Army has a very important class that they bore in to your brain constantly called Operation Security or OPSEC. It basically teaches you not to tell anyone or post on social media about troop or equipment movement, times, or sizes. This is something I kept in mind on my calls home. Renee answered "hey baby." She said very excitedly. I said "hey baby cakes" as the screen slowly focused to bring in a more clear video. When the camera focused in she was sitting on the coach smoking a cigarette. I said "I see how it is you just lounge around when I leave." She said "yep" then she yelled "kids come here daddy is on the phone." I was so happy to see all of them and they were pretty happy to see me. We asked about each other's day and how everything was going. Then she asked "when will you be leaving for Korea?" I lied and said "not sure yet. I will let you know when we get there though." She rolled her eyes, but she knew I couldn't talk about it. We talked a while about the kids starting back to school and how all of that was going. Everything was going good thank God. I would get pretty stressed if something was happening at home and I couldn't help out with or control, so Renee wouldn't ever tell me the small stuff she knew would bother me.

The next week went by in a blur, between training in the day and talking to Renee and the kids each night for about 30 mins. It was finally time to get on the plane and fly into Korea.

I had painted a picture in my mind of what kind of situation we would be dropped into. This always helped me all through my career (expect the worse and you will be prepared for it. Then if it ain't as bad as you imagined, well you had a win right off the bat.) I also learned to always be positive and hunt the good things no matter how bad it was. I said to myself "How bad can it get?"

I decided to pull up google and I typed in the Search bar "Korean war 2018 Predictions." All kinds of links come up. I decided to pick the News Week one and see what they thought.

The experts with all of the college degrees said" in order to eliminate Korea's nuclear arsenal it would be better to do a ground invasion instead of an air attack." I personally would not like to a ground invasion since it is rumored that all of North Korea's civilians believe we are the devil and nothing but pure evil and they need to destroy us at all cost. I mean even in Iraq there was peaceful citizens. Could we fight the whole country of North Korea if civilians jumped in? The also predict the deaths to be over 20,000 per day. I figured that was all I could read for the night. I guess it was going to be bad as I imagined.

Chapter 10: Starting in Korea

We landed in Seoul Airport in South Korea about 50 miles from the border and about 10 miles from where we would be stationed in our tiny base. I was pretty nervous, and my Soldiers were too. Neither one of us would admit it though.

On the ride from the airport we traveled in troop carriers or cargo trucks as some call them. The Army calls them a Light Medium Tactical Vehicle LMTV's or a 5 ton. I am sure you have seen a few on the highway before. They are pretty big and usually tan or camo, with a tarp over the bed kind of like a covered wagon. I always thought it was funny that they have light in their name considering they weigh almost 13 ton and are capable of hauling 5 tons of cargo.

While we rode to the site no one really talked. I think it was mainly because it is so loud in the bed of the truck. I will never forget the smell. We had a tarp over the bed and it was closed so we never really seen anything driving in, but the smell...ugh. The smell of burning tires and human flesh.

It reminded me of the first time I was dispatched to a car fire when I was a volunteer fire fighter in my teenage years. This would be the first time I actually smelled a human body burning. The smell seems to stick in your nose for days. It was an elderly lady that had ran off the road and the car burst into flames before anyone even had time to get her out she burnt up in the car. A witness at the scene said she had to be unconscious because she never made a sound. That kind of made me feel better about the thing.

When we got to where we were going we had arrived at a small American Military base called Camp Howze in Bongilchon,

South Korea. I couldn't tell a whole lot about it because it was dark. Our rooms were two man rooms that barely had enough room for a set of bunk beds and two wall lockers to put all of our gear in. From the outside it looked like a conex which is the big shipping containers you see on cargo ships in the movies or on the news. Ours were desert tan on the outside with a small white door that seemed to be made out of paneling. When we stepped inside the walls were a light blue color and the celling was white with one light in the middle of the room. The floors were white faded ceramic tile with black trim that went all around the room. The bunk beds were made out of some kind of light colored wood, my guess would be pine. Then the wall lockers were a darker color of wood like oak. It was no mansion, but it was where I would be living for the next year and it could have been a whole lot worse.

We bedded down for the night to get some sleep. I figured I would look into the internet situation tomorrow and see what was close by store wise. I woke up around 0600 as daylight was starting to ease into our side of the world. I stepped outside to see what this place looked like.

Camp Howze was closed down back in 2004 and turned it over to the South Korean Army in 2005. I guess we had kind of borrowed it again to set up a large detainee housing facility. Most of the structures or building were pretty ran down, but there was all kinds of new chain link fence and Constantine wire (C wire). There was a lot of construction going on all over the camp. Seems like we were going to end up building a majority of the prison around the detainees as they were brought in.

SFC Booker was outside drinking coffee as always. I seriously think I seen him drink water one time in the 5 years I knew him. I said "what do you think SFC?" He said "this is a nice place. Most of you all wouldn't make it in the shit holes I have stayed in." I said "roger SFC. I meant what do you think about the prison?" He said "it will work because we will make it work. It will be hard but it will be ok if I can toughen you wimps up!" He wasn't in a bad mood I just think he was angry about what Soldiers had become over the last few years. At least I always knew what he was thinking I guess.

The first few days we were helping the engineers put up more C wire and installing gates and fences around the compound. We still didn't have much internet, but we had a satellite phone so I planned on calling Renee soon. I hadn't talked to her in 3 days since we arrived and I knew she would be worried. I got to talking to Southern and he mentioned there was a little calling trailer across the base we could go to so we did. It was a small trailer like the shower one in Kuwait, but It had about 6 pay phones inside of it that you could use a phone card to call with. I dug in my uniform for the phone card Renee had bought me. I said "Damn! I forgot my card." Southern handed me his without hesitation. He said "here use mine." I asked "are you sure?" He said yeah don't use my whole 500 minutes though ha-ha." I said "I won't and thank you so much man." Southern done stuff like that all the time. He really was a nice guy he just had to play tough so people wouldn't ask him for favors or dumb stuff is what he always said anyways.

The phone rang a few times and my heart was sinking lower with each ring. I was scared Renee wouldn't answer and there is no telling when I would be able to come back over and call again. Finally she answered I said "thank God." She said "what's wrong?" I said "nothing I was just afraid you wasn't going

to answer." She said "I was worried something happened to you."
I said "no, just traveling here and getting everything set up. There
is no internet yet." She said "oh" I said "yeah, and Southern
showed me this phone trailer and even let me borrow his card."
She asked "isn't that the one you said acted like a cocky hard ass."
I said "yep, I am softening him up." She laughed a little which
really made my day. We talked about the kids and how everything
was and then I told her "I gotta go internet should be working in a
couple of weeks and maybe we could video chat." She said "of
course" in a really excited voice. She Said "The news mentioned
there is a lot of fighting and bombing next to the border is that
close to you?" there was a bit of a pause, then I said "the news
just adds to shit to get ratings honey. You can't listen to them."
She said "you be careful. I don't need a hero I need you to come
home." I said "I will be....good bye honey." She said "good bye."

We stayed so busy the next few weeks I didn't have time
to think. We almost had the TIF finished it was designed to hold
roughly 2500 detainees and we wanted to build it to hold another
1000. Apparently the people that out ranked me thought there
would be a lot of Koreans captured or maybe they surrender. I for
one knew these people were not going to surrender they were
going to stand their ground and fight to the death. No giving up
and no surrendering.

By this time a lot of the Soldier's nerves had calmed a bit
we got used to the random mortar or rocket going off just a few
yards outside of our base. Luckily we had the phalanx gun that
was an anti-ship missile and mortar gun. Basically it would shoot a
cluster of fire like a firework and it would cause the mortar or
rocket to explode. It was our saving grace in a lot of instances.

Eventually we got Wi-Fi on the whole compound. It wasn't lightning fast, but it worked well enough to video chat with my family. Which absolutely tickled me to death.

Chapter 11: My First Mission

The time came to start going out and clearing certain towns that were just north of the border. Basically, we would do a random sweep twice a week in the middle of the night. We were looking for any weapons or threats that may lead to a loss of Soldier lives. We were on a rotation the first night would be 1st and 2nd platoon's night and the second night would be 3rd and 4th platoon's night. These areas we were clearing would make it possible to set up a forward operating base (FOB) north of the boarder and close in on the remaining enemy. These areas would later be labeled as the "Green Zone" or safety zone, meaning it was a safe area to retreat to if stuff got really bad.

The first night was my platoons, SGT Southern and I were readying our Soldier's going over pre-combat checks and pre-combat inspections. PCC's and PCI's is what the Army calls it, basically make sure your soldier's had all of their gear and equipment. I had some Five Finger Death Punch playing on my IPod to get the guys pumped. Our team was ready to go. We mounted up in our 4 door up armored 1165 HMMWV (High Mobility Multipurpose Wheeled Vehicle). Southern and his team would be in the lead vehicle and my team and I would take the rear of the 4 Humvee convoy. Twenty Soldier's rolling through the night not knowing what was going to happen in the next second or how many was coming back, and it is a night I would never forget.

SPC Perkins was my driver, SPC Swann was the gunner, I was the Radio Operator/ Truck Commander (TC), and we had to haul the interpreter which was a South Korean Soldier named something I couldn't pronounce that started with a B so we just called him bravo, and we had a new kid that was our combat medic SPC Rashaan or Money as we called him, because he was always talking about spending money on stuff like Jet skis, trucks, motorcycles, and fast cars. I didn't know much about him he was in his early twenties and never said much.

We headed for Kaesong, North Korea it used to be a large industrial area. It was one of the closest towns to the border and once employed both North and South Koreans, but due to the constant

arguing back and forth between the governments it was shut down in February of 2016. The army really wanted control of it. It would be a good step towards the North for us.

After the bombings and the Infantry had swept through the area there wasn't a whole lot left. Some structures were still partially standing. It was just a bunch of old abandoned factories, and small houses that wrapped around what was once a small industrial town. It was a wreck and smelled like an erupted sewage plant. The moon was full that night so there was quite a bright loom. You could see a good twenty to 30 yards in front of you. At the time I wasn't quite sure if that was a good thing or a bad thing. Our mission would be to search buildings and homes making sure no one was breaking the Law or trying to set up an ambush to take out U.S. Soldier's

We parked just outside of town, just in case there was some combative enemies in the area we didn't want to roll through like the cavalry, and let them know we were there. We broke down in our teams and designated what team was clearing which buildings. I think there was like 20 buildings and my team needed to clear the North 5. This doesn't seem like a lot but 3 were factory buildings which meant when you come through the door there was one big wide open room and plenty of hiding places amongst the machinery and debris. Then the other 2 building were small homes that were three story square shaped buildings. These were broken down into small apartments so each floor was an apartment for a small family. Most of these houses were set up with a kitchen, living room, then a small bedroom, and bathroom. That is 3 rooms per floor. That gets pretty hairy...one mistake and we could be in a big mess quick. All of the houses had narrow entrances, and small living rooms. So we could burst in on someone ready for us and not have anywhere to go but through them.

We started with the 3 factory buildings first. The rule always is once you hit the door you go in fast and silent that is until the first shot is fired, then it was time to get loud. Make it sound like you had a hundred guys with you. This sometimes would make the enemy lay down arms and surrender in Iraq. So far in Korea we did not know if it was going to work or not, but it is how we were trained. We stacked on the door Perkins was our point man meaning he would be the first one in. I was second, Swann was third, the interpreter would wait outside and Money would pull rear security as the 4th man. Considering only half of this building was standing I felt like we had an advantage.

Perkins went through the door like a fox fast and silent. It was odd considering the size of the man. Swann, and I was right on his heals Perkins went left, I went right and Swann filled in the gap between the 2 of us. It was smooth and flawless just like we had trained. There was a lot of old machines and other stuff to maneuver around, and all kinds of places for the enemy to hide. Plenty of dark corners I wanted to point my weapon and flashlight on, but I didn't. We all whispered clear about the same time. Then moved out of the factory and on to the next. The next was half demolished as well and just like the first fast and smooth "all clear". We were about to stack on the third and a shot rang out in another building, and then two more followed. It was Southern's Platoon, I couldn't help but wonder if he was alright. I didn't have time to think about it much because we were stacked up on the final factory and we still had two more houses to search. Since the shot had been fired I am sure anyone within a mile would be headed this way. This upped our tempo, we had to be faster and get these buildings clear before the ambush closed in, which is if there was one.

The third factory still had about 90% of it standing, this one would be a bit trickier. Instead of clearing half of a building we were clearing a whole one. Which meant more places for the enemy to hide and jump out of firing before we could even see them. We burst in not caring about sound or stealth any more. Lights shinning everywhere sounding off with "Clear" "Moving" "Clear" moving like gears on a properly greased machine. "All Clear" "Just two buildings more guys we got this" I said as we headed towards the other two buildings. Each building was no more than 30ft apart, but moving up to the houses we were going to have to move across a 60ft clearing. I felt a little uneasy about the whole thing.

As we moved across the clearing a shot rang out splitting the dirt behind our rear man Money. Perkins shouted "Shots 12 o'clock 30 meters 2nd story window." Letting the rest of us know where the shot came from. We doubled our smooth pace and tried to maintain formation. Another rang out about the time we stacked on the door. This one was no doubt coming from the second floor it struck about a foot from Swann's feet. We cleared the first floor in seconds it seemed.

Then we stacked back up on the rear of the building where the metal stairwell was leading up to the second floor. We moved up the stairwell as a solid unit. Stacking a few inches off the wall at the top. The door was locked tight and dead bolted I imagine. It was our rear man Money's job to come around and break the door open with a sledge hammer. One solid blow just below the knob and the door crumbled splitting it almost in half. Without hesitation Perkins went in, then me, and then Swann. Perkins went to the right slamming what was left of the door against the wall to make sure no one was behind it. Then he followed the wall down to the corner. I swung in left running down to the end of the first wall then rotated inward towards a dark corner. Swann swung in the middle a shot fired I saw the muzzle flash just before my light found the Korean man standing in the corner of the living room. The shot chewed holes in the wall beside me and somehow manage to miss me. I then took aim and squeezed off two rounds at his chest. Perkins then fired one more towards his mid-section. He fell limp and motionless we shouted "CLEAR." Then cleared the bed room and bathroom "ALL CLEAR". We stopped for a second to check each other for gunshot wounds no one was hit. We assessed the Korean's corps.

Sure enough all three shots found their mark two entered the center of his chest and the third entered about the middle of his ribs on the left side. It was a middle aged man with clean cut hair and a short goatee, he was wearing a faded blue button up shirt that was unbuttoned exposing his white V-neck shirt underneath. Then he had on black denim pants, and black lace up work boots. He just laid there lifeless the three holes in his V-neck shirt leaked blood that ran all down his belly and on to his black pants. His eyes were half way closed, but filled with emptiness.

I just stared thinking I did this. I took this man's life. I kept telling myself I had no choice. I have to get home to my family. What if he had a family? What if he was doing this so he could get home to them? What if this was his home and they evacuated to China to avoid the bombings? What if the bombings killed everyone he loved and he was the only survivor? So many things raced through my head along with the adrenaline it was enough to make me a little dizzy. Then I noticed we were all shaking after what just happened. Perkins asked "are you ok SGT?" I said "Yeah, what about y'all." They said "yeah" I said "let's clear this last one then."

We exited the building a little slower this time maybe because the adrenaline was winding down or maybe because everyone was thinking of that guy. Either way I think it bothered us all. We stacked up on the final building moving a bit slower and more carefully. I guess reality had hit letting us know this is no game, and that we could actually die. We cleared the building without any issues and headed over to the collection point.

When we got there we heard some paining yells like someone was dying. I shifted back and forth through the crowd, it was Southern he was lying on a stretcher or litter as the Army calls it. His clothes were badly stained with blood, which I hope none of it was his. He was holding his side just above his waist line where the medic had just applied a pressure dressing, and the blood was already seeping through.

The Individual body armor (IBA) does not protect the Soldiers sides or ribs area too well. It has good plates in the front and back, but nothing much to protect the sides or rib area. We sat him in the back of a Humvee and I jumped in there with him. I didn't care what anyone said I wasn't leaving his side. I held his hand and asked "what the hell happened?" He said I was the first one through the door and he fired from my 3 o'clock position and I caught one just above the hip. I got the bastard though, shot him right in the throat. He was choking on his own blood for a few seconds before he finally died. Stupid Bastard!" I said "I am glad you got him." He said I heard shots up your way. All of yours ok?" I said "yeah we are good. We got him, Asshole was up on the second floor backed in a corner. He about got me." The blood started to stain his lips, which meant the bullet had passed through his stomach or digestive track I thought "that isn't good." He said "It isn't like you think…." I asked "What isn't?" He said "being shot…..it is like someone opened the door on your body and let the cold air in, but just in that one spot. I said "that's pretty weird man." He asked "Am I dying?" I said "why hell no. you're staying with me buddy." He said "good I would hate to tell you my last words you prick." I said "me too I don't even like you." The joking seemed to lighten the mood, but I had no clue if he would live or die. That was up to the Lord at this point.

We made it back to base and by this time the blood was running down his cheek in a thin stream. He said hold on to this for me. It was his letters home he had written for a situation like this. I said "I am just holding them until you get back to base." The Army doctors rushed him back to the ER. I walked out of the hospital and got in the Humvee. I just stared at the blood that was all over my hands. I thought "what will I do if he dies this is my best friend and roommate. What will his wife do? I felt so awful. Flashes of the Korean that I killed earlier that night and what I had just witnessed with Southern kept going through my head. It was almost unbearable. I decided to have a smoke. I used water from my canteen to halfway wash the blood off and then dried my hands on my pants. I lit my cigarette then immediately threw up. Maybe it was the taste of the first puff, maybe it was all that was on my mind. The sick feeling went away after I threw up and I felt a little better, but I still couldn't finish my cigarette so I flipped the fire from the end and put the butt in my pocket. This was how we usually put out cigarettes in the Army. The ride back to base was a blur I was in and out of sleep and in a daze. I was sick with worry and anger. Why did it have to be him? Why did it have to be anyone really?

Not long after I made it back to my tent SFC Booker came in and asked me how I was doing. I said "good I guess." Then he said words I will never forget "the call just came in and….Southern didn't make it." I was over whelmed by all of the emotions. I wanted to cry, but I couldn't seem to get a tear to come out. My throat was burning, and I was so tired and angry. SFC Booker said "I know it is tough losing a fellow comrade that you were so close to. Sadly that is a part of this job. I have lost a lot of fellow Soldier's in battle throughout my 20 years. To be honest it will get easier eventually, even though right now it doesn't seem it ever will. I will leave you be now." I said "I appreciate it Sergeant." It was the first time I seen him show any emotion for anything. He said "take two days off and get yourself together." I said "Roger Sergeant" as I laid down on my cot.

Chapter 12: The Next Few Days

I tossed and turned most of the night. To be honest I don't think I ever actually fell asleep. Every time I closed my eyes I saw Southern or the Korean man. I finally gave up around 8 am and got out of bed. I figured I would pack up some of Southern's things. I mean I wouldn't want someone else going through my stuff. I got me a piece of paper to start a hand jammed inventory sheet of all of his gear and personal belongings. I started packing up the drawers first. I packed the shirts away, and then wrote down how many there were. Then in the bottom of his shirt drawer there was a composition book it simply said "SGT Southern" on the front. I picked it up and an envelope and blue confetti fell out on the floor. The envelope had a card inside. I slid the card out and on the front in big bold letters it said "It's a Boy". I immediately felt sick. I opened it and sure enough there was an ultra sound image inside that said "boy" just off to the side of the image.

Southern was going to be a dad! All this time he had been trying and he finally got his wish, but he would never meet the little guy. This made me think of my children and what they would do if I ended up like Southern. I sat down on my bunk and cried like a baby. I had to call my family. I had to hear their voices. What time was it back home? 2am! That won't work. I will have to wait until tonight to call them. The supply team came in to do the inventory. So I got out of their way, besides I had a mission. I had a letter to mail home to a Southard's wife. I headed to the mail room to drop the letter. I wanted to open it I wanted to let her know how sincerely sorry I was and how I felt.

I could picture Southern's wife sitting on the couch. A blue government Dodge Caravan would pull in the driveway, two military men would get out in their blue dress uniform, and come up to the door. They would ring the door bell, and wait on her to answer. As soon as she opens the door to these two men she would know that her Southern wouldn't be coming home. That her baby would never meet his father. She would step back and put her hand over her mouth saying "No….please…..No Not my Cody….. No!! They would give their usual scripted speech that they have told hundreds of family members over the years.

"I am Staff Sergeant Scott Eckard with the 110 Military Police Battalion, from Fort Bragg, North Carolina. Are you Leslie Southern? Are you the wife of Sergeant Cody Southern? I have an important message to deliver from the Secretary of the Army, may we come in, Mrs. Southern? (Once inside one would say) The Secretary of the Army has asked me to express his deep regret that your husband, SGT Cody Southern died in a military hospital in Camp Howze, South Korea from injuries sustained in battle on August 5, 2018. The Secretary extends his deepest sympathy to you and your family in your tragic loss."

Then the two Soldier's would leave. The next few days leading up to the funeral would be the toughest. No 24 year old woman that is 4 months pregnant should have to plan her husband's funeral.

Southern's body would be transported in an 18 gauge black steel Army casket. He would be escorted from the hospital in South Korea all the way to the local funeral home in Western NC, never leaving sight of a Soldier except when in the belly of the airplane. Once his body makes it to the local funeral home it will be under 24 hour guard until the burial. The Honor guard would be deployed generally ten Soldier's to conduct the funeral honors. Taps would play then the Soldier's would do the 21 gun salute, then two Soldier's would remove the flag from the casket and fold it. A Soldier would present the flag to his wife and say: **"On behalf of the President of the United States, the United States Army, and a grateful Nation, please accept this flag as a symbol of our appreciation for your loved one's honorable and faithful service.**

It was killing me just thinking about all of this taking place and how his poor wife would feel. I didn't know how to help her or what to do. I was depressed for the first time in my life I felt completely helpless.

That night was another sleepless one just waiting til 1 am so I can call home. It would be 6 pm back home and Renee should be home from work. I decided to call instead of video chatting, that way Renee wouldn't see my zombie like face from my sickening nerve problems, and sleepless nights. She answered almost immediately. "Hello" I said "hey baby" trying to talk like everything was fine. She asked "is everything ok? You didn't video chat me like usual." I lied and said "the internet has been down." She said "ohhh….Are you ok." I lied and said "yeah, and you?" trying to get her to talk so I didn't have to. She said "pretty good, just missing my honey." I said "I miss all of you more than you know. I want to come home I am done with this place." She said "it won't be much longer honey." We talked a while about the kids and how everyone was. Then she asked me what I had prayed she wouldn't. She asked "well how is Southern?" I couldn't tell her he had died on the same mission I was on. I couldn't say I had to kill a man so I could live. I lied and said "he is asleep." She said "ok…are you sure you are ok." I said "yes baby I just miss you all and we been working long shifts." She said "I am worried about you." I said "I am fine honey don't worry about me. I gotta go ok. Love you bye."

Did she see right through my lies? Did she know I was hiding something? I don't know I just knew I couldn't tell her the truth right now. I would tell her when I got home. I loved her so much and hating lying, but it was for the best, or so I thought.

Chapter 13: Going Home

The next couple of months kind of drug by, but I was getting closer to going home. I could finally hold my kids and kiss my wife. It was just a couple of weeks away now. I started to doubt ever making it home. After Southern I hadn't really told anyone, but I was hurting emotionally and mentally. Demons that were all so familiar from my first deployment had come back to haunt me. I kept thinking "maybe I am supposed to die over here. Maybe it is not meant for me to go home this way." With each mission and each close call the excitement of going home faded slowly from my mind. The excitement was replaced with dread. How was I supposed to function in the civilian world like this? How am I supposed to be a father when I can barely stand to look in the mirror? Does my family even miss me? Will my son remember me? Will my family care that I am home? Who had I become? A killer a murderer of family men that was doing what they thought was right to protect their home, their family, and their country. How was these men different from me? I would do the same if someone attacked the U.S. and came knocking on my door to search my house. Yes, I have guns in my house! Yes, I would defend what is mine! I guess I would be shot in a room clearing shoot out too. So I guess I am not that different from my enemy.

The day finally came to go home. A bus would be arriving any minute to take us to the airport. We would ride the plane into Fort Dix, NJ and stay there a few days to make sure we were ok to go back to our old lives. Was I ready? What if they kept me in Fort Dix as some science experiment in a padded room all day getting my food from a slot in a big metal door?

I thought "you will be fine stay calm". I went into a room where you sit with a doctor and they asked me a lot of questions no one wants to answer. A lot of them were "do you feel like you are ready to go back to civilian life?" I felt like a prisoner being set free after serving my sentence. I gave text book answers to each question. I knew what they wanted to hear and I didn't want to be there any longer than I had to. Then came the curve ball. The doctor read to me the commanders notes. Then the doctor asked "did you lose any fellow Soldiers while deployed?" I am sure he could tell this made me uncomfortable. My palms started sweating immediately. I said "yes, my roommate Southern." He asked "how are you doing with that." I said "fine" He asked "how are you sleeping? Do you fall asleep ok?" I said "most nights I reckon." He asked "Have you ever used anything to help you go to sleep." I asked "you mean counting sheep and shit like that?" That kind of made him back off. He finally said I could go. I was so happy to get out of there.

We flew into an airport in the mountains just outside of the city. It was so beautiful descending to the airport not far above the tops of the mountains. After you get beneath the clouds you can she each and every shadow the clouds cast on to the surface of the earth, and it is amazing. It was a warm summer day as we landed there were two fire trucks parked on each side of the run way spraying their hoses in the air across the airplane. It was pretty cool. Then the plane made a right turn on the run way. That is when we came in sight of all of the families that were waiting at the gate.

They were holding their banners and cheering "Welcome Home." We all stood up to collect our carry-on bags from the overhead compartments. I couldn't help but thinking "I wish Southern could be here for this. Please lord help his poor wife." I was one of the last ones to get off the plane. A lot of Soldier's were already holding and hugging their family members and so happy, the crowd erupted with cheers of happiness as we walked across the tarmac. I began to look for Renee and the kids. I walked through the crowd. Where could they be? Maybe they had car trouble? With ever yell of daddy I turned and looked, but it wasn't them. Finally I saw my Renee standing off to herself with her hand on her forehead to block out the sun so she could see further. She saw me and headed my way. She was more beautiful than I remembered she had a fresh short haircut. It was spiked a little in the back and nice dark eyeliner that made her eyes pop in the evening sun. Then she had on those nice tight white pants that I loved so much. She even had on my favorite low cut blouse. YES, I am the luckiest man in the world! Then bang a little boy ran into my leg. I looked down IT WAS MY BOY! It was my little Jay Bird. I grabbed him up, he was so big had he really grown that much? WOW!! He was heavier than I remember too. He said "I Wove you daddy" in that cute little boy voice. I have never hugged anyone as hard as I hugged him that day. Then two more bumped into my hips and back. It was Hadley and Emma they were so happy and hugging me. I about squeezed them to death. We just kept saying "I love you and I miss you." I sat Jay down just in time to grab Renee around the waste. I gave her a long hug and kissed her probably a thousand times. Was this all real? Was I really home? We all pitched in and carried my stuff to the car. I said "goodbye to my fellow Soldier's" It would be 90 days before I seen a lot of them again. Some of them it would be the last time.

We went to a restaurant to celebrate me coming home. On the way there Emma asked me if I still had the card. I asked "what card?" acting like I didn't know what she meant. She said "the Joker one that looked like you that I gave you for good luck. I said "Oh! This one?" as I pulled it from my breast pocket. She yelled "you still have it." I said "yep, gotta hold on to my good luck charm."

The restaurant was a buffet place just inside the city. My

dad, brother, and mom surprised me by meeting us there. I was so happy to see them, but not nearly as happy as they were to see me apparently.

We got our food and took our seats. I usually helped with little man's stuff, but Renee said she would get it. My brother said "let's pray before we eat." We all held hands and bowed our heads as he said *"our heavenly father as we come to you today we would like to thank you for safely bringing my brother home to us. We would like to ask for protection for the Soldier's still fighting, Lord we would like to thank you for bringing us together and keeping us safe in our many travels. Thank you for this meal and this day Lord AMEN." I quickly added "please be with the family members of the ones that didn't make it home AMEN."*

I looked up and everyone was staring at me. I said "let's eat." The table we had sat down at had me positioned where I had my back to the entrance door and the kitchen staff were walking back and forth behind me carrying drinks and plate of food. There was 11 of us so it would be hard to get another table somewhere else in the restaurant. I asked the waitress "can we sit somewhere else?" My dad asked "what's wrong with this table son?" I said "nothing I just want to move! I want to see the door!" Another waitress walking by with a stack of plates and dropped 3 of them, they went crashing to the floor. I screamed "Damn it!" and dove to the floor. Everyone in the restaurant was staring in silence at this point. I got up embarrassed and said "I am going to smoke."

Renee followed me out "are you ok honey?" She asked. I said "I'm fine" She said "no you're not." I said "well jumping like that embarrassed me." She said "look at me." She placed a hand on each side of my cheeks she said "you just came home from a warzone honey that is nothing to be embarrassed of." I pulled away and lit my cigarette. I said "I will be fine. Can't we just get a burger at a drive through and go home?" She said "yeah if that is what you want." I said "well that is what I want." I thought "what is wrong with me?" I wish there was someone I could talk to I wish I could just pick up the phone and call Southern. I sucked down my cigarette and flipped the butt to the curb.

We got in the car and headed home. I said "I need to grab something at the store." Renee asked "what?" I said "a beer" she said "ok" I figured she would fuss, but she didn't. I kept thinking I will be ok when I get home and have a beer then everything will be fine.

We got home and the kids had made me a banner "welcome home daddy!" it hit me right in the feelings. I suddenly felt a little happiness. I apologized to the kids. I said "I am sorry for walking out of the restaurant I just get a little nervous around a lot of people." They said "its ok we love you daddy." I said "I love you all too." My family visited for a few hours and talked I probably had 10 beers in just a few hours. They got ready to leave and my brother said "take care of yourself, and don't drink too much." I said "hell I am grown I will be ok." It kind of bothered him seeing me drink like that. I hugged all of them and told them safe travels. I told all of them I loved them and how much I care about them in some slurred words Renee later told me.

That night was rough. I kissed all the kids and told them "good night I Love you." They headed off to bed. I laid down and I kept feeling like I was missing something. I got up and got a drink of water. I talked to Renee a minute and kissed her good night. She asked "are you ok." I said "there is something I need to do, but I don't want you to think I am crazy." I had got used to going to sleeping with my M4 beside my bed just in arms reach. I needed that weapon by my side. I got up made sure my shotgun was unloaded and propped it next to my bed. I said "there that is better." She said jokingly "you need help." I said "yeah" and giggled. I couldn't let her know that I was scared of what each day forward would bring. I was scared of how I would react to everything most people face each day.

The next day I got up and woke Emma up to get ready for school. I turned on her bedroom light and said "time to get up honey." Then I walked into the kitchen to start the coffee pot. I went back in her room to make sure she was up. I said "Emma come on get up honey." She kind of rolled over slowly. So I turned on the T.V. and watched it for a few minutes…..still no Emma. I went in there. I shouted "EMMA GET UP NOW!!!" I walked over and jerked the covers down and said "LETS GO!" I grabbed her by the arm and pulled her up. She let out a scream "your hurting my arm" I looked at her and she was scared to death. I let her go and said calmly "Please get ready." She said "ok" and quickly grabbed her shoes. My daughter was scared of me. What kind of man scares his daughter like that? I shouldn't be a father. Poor ole Southern couldn't make it home he would have been a great father, and I made it for some reason. "I ain't worth a shit." I thought. I took Emma to school and on the way I told her "I am sorry I hurt your arm." She looked down and rubbed her arm she said "its ok I know you didn't mean to." "That's right I didn't mean to" I thought, or did I? Did I hurt my daughter on purpose? Am I some kind of monster? I dropped her off and went back home. I was still off work for another week, so I decided to take care of some stuff around home. I took Jay and went to the tag office to renew my inspection and tag. Everything went quite smooth with the process though it used to be an all-day affair. I even bumped into an old friend from high school and spoke to him a few minutes. It felt good to catch up. We talked about our high school years and good memories.

We finished up and went our separate ways. I walked up the street and he headed down the street. On my way in I noticed there was a dumpster in the alley just next door to the tag office. They were remodeling a building on the second story. About the time I walked by with Jay holding my hand. Someone threw some debris from the second story into that dumpster. BAM!! I jumped grabbed Jay and ran over to the other side of the car parked in the alley yelling "GET DOWN GET DOWN!!!! Everyone in the street just stared. I even heard one person say "what's wrong with that guy?" another said "that's what drugs do for ya." To be honest I wish it was drugs. That would mean eventually they would wear off instead of living this nightmare every day. Jay said "that was fun daddy do it again." I said "that's enough fun for one day buddy."

Chapter 14: Visiting Her

After about a week of being home. I kept thinking of Southern's wife and I decided to look her up and pay her a visit. That is if she would even agree to meet with me. The only way I knew how to find her is through Facebook. I typed her name in and sent her a message. I said "I don't know if you ever heard of me, but I was a good friend of your husbands and his roommate. I would like to meet with you and talk to you if you want. She almost instantly messaged me back and said "I would love to meet and talk to you."

We agreed to meet a little diner just outside of the city. I got there a few minutes early to get a seat where I wanted, so hopefully I wouldn't make another scene like in the last restaurant. She walked in the diner and I raised my hand so she could see me. When she rounded the corner an infant car seat came into site. I didn't know whether to be happy or to cry. She said "Hi I'm Leslie." I said "Hi and introduced myself."

Leslie was a petite blonde that had short hair and green eyes. She looked much different from the photo Cody carried. She looked older more tired and less perky. I said "is this the little guy?" She said "yes, this is Cody Southern Jr. there was a little brown headed fella that looked just like his father in that car seat. He was smiling a big smile. I felt some tears coming on so I quickly asked "Would you like a coffee? I need a coffee." We ordered a coffee each and she took out the baby's bottle and gave it to him. He smiled even bigger. I couldn't look at him anymore. She said "Cody mentioned you from time to time. He really liked you, and cared about you." I said "he was the best." Then she jumped to the question that she had rolled around in her head for months. She asked "were you there that night." I said "yes, sadly." She asked "What happened?"

I said "well we were on a mission just north of the border and we were clearing buildings. I went with my team and Southern went with his. They kicked in a door and Southern rushed in just as a Korean Local was opening fire. He caught one round just above his hip. I rode with him to the hospital. We got there and they wheeled him back and that was the last time I seen him." I had tears in my eyes. I was trying to fight them back but I just couldn't. Her cheeks were soaked by her tears. She said "thanks for telling me." I said "I am so sorry for your loss and I hope you know if there is anything you need you can call me." we talked for a while about how things were going and told stories about him. It kind of helped take some of the weight off my shoulders I had been carrying. I got home and Renee was there. She asked "what did you do today?" I said "I visited Southern's wife Leslie." She said "How is she doing with everything now that he is gone." I said "good I guess….wait. How did you know he passed away?" She said "it was all over the news just a few nights after we talked on the phone and you told me he was asleep." I said "Renee I couldn't tell you." She said "let me guess to protect me?" I opened the fridge and grabbed a beer. She said sarcastically "it is three o'clock are you thirsty?" I said "yeah maybe a little." I opened the fridge and grabbed two more. I said "I will be in the wood shop if you need me." I went to the shop and slammed the door, I turned some Avenged Sevenfold high as my radio would go. Why were we arguing all the time? Why couldn't she understand I can't tell her everything? I just wish she could know how I feel!

Chapter 15: Living with my Demons

It is not easy coming home from a war zone and the friends you see every day and talk to everyday are not there anymore. In the National Guard you get a 90 day break from the day you come home til the time you have to report again. Then you have to go through three yellow ribbon ceremonies. At these yellow ribbon programs they evaluate you and see how well your transition back to civilian life is going. Some people don't even make it to the first yellow ribbon. Instead they end up in jail or take their own life.

Things wasn't the same as I had left them at home, that added a lot more stress to mine and Renee's relationship. The kids didn't listen to me the way they used to. If they were hurt or having a bad day they wanted momma to kiss it and make it better, or listen to their problems. It was like I was a ghost. It is a horrible feeling when your kids don't feel comfortable with telling you what they are going through. Maybe it was my fault. I had gotten used to telling a Soldier to do something and they would jump up and do it. My kids huffed and puffed and moved like pond water. This mad me so angry, But should it? Was that normal?

I had made it a point to contact the Soldier's in my Platoon at least once a week and talk for a few minutes. It is called a buddy check and it is strongly recommended in the military. I called Swann one Friday evening no answer. I called the next day straight to voicemail. Then later that evening I got a phone call from SFC D. He informed me that SPC Swann's wife had left him yesterday and he had taken his own life. Sadly this happens with 22 veterans everyday. I called Perkins to check on him and let him know the news. We stayed on the phone and talked for some time after that. We talked about our everyday troubles, and what we were going through. Sometime all it takes is someone that knows what you have been through and someone that can listen that understands.

He said "He couldn't even watch fire works with his family. I said "Yea I stay away from those. Someone shot some off at the lake and I couldn't stick around to watch them. I almost freaked out. He said "yeah me too." I then admitted to him I had been drinking about a 12 pack a day. This was very alarming to Perkins. He said "Sergeant have you thought about talking to someone." I laughed and said "no it is just to help me sleep man." He said "if you have trouble sleeping you might need to call behavioral health." I said "No I am good what are you damn doctor?" He said "no I am just looking out for you." I said "thanks, but I am fine….besides they might lock me up and throw away the key." We said bye and hung up.

It was about 5 o'clock in the evening. I had to have a drink. I asked Renee "Need anything from the store? I am going to get some beer?" she looked at me with disgust and said "no, just go on." I went to the store and grabbed a case. I came back home told her that Swann had taken his life, and I was going to build a fire in the fire pit out back and that I would be out there with my beer if she needed me. She said "you need help or you are going to end up like Swann". This made me angry I said "maybe that's not such a bad thing as I stomped out.

I woke up the next morning around 5 am froze half to death. The big fire from the night before had died down to just a few ambers. I am guessing I fell asleep in my chair. What is that noise? It was my cellphone ringing I answered it…"Hello" the person on the other end said "Hello son. Are you up?" It took me a second to realize it, but it was my dad. I said "why yeah are you?" I sat up in my chair and started to dig in the pocket of my jeans for my pack of cigarettes. I don't know if dad was just bored or if Renee told him what had been going on, but had called to see if I wanted to do some rabbit hunting. I used to love rabbit hunting we used to go all the time when I was a kid. I said "sure" I got up out of my chair I was so stiff and sore I could barely move. "How much did I drink?" There was a pile of beer cans at my feet. Whew! My head is killing me! I went inside Renee and the kids were still asleep. I accidently woke her grabbing a couple of things to get ready to go. She asked "what are you doing?" I said "going hunting with dad." She said "be careful I love you" I kissed her and said "I will." I met dad just a mile or two from the game lands on the far side of the county. All the way there all I could think about was Swann. "Why did he do it?" I could never do that, could I?

I got in the truck and dad asked "how ya been?" I said "pretty good and you?" He said "you still drinking a lot? You look rough!" I said "yeah I had a few last night." He just shook his head and said "that will kill you ya know." I said "hopefully not." We got over to the hunting area and turned the dogs out. Dad said "I hate to ask but me and your brother were talking and...you ain't going to shoot me if I shoot at the rabbit are you." I said "why no. I might just jump a little." He said "ok" with a lot of uncertainty in his voice.

The dogs started barking and dad said "it is jumped look for it." I said "ok". The dogs ran it right to him "BOOM" the shotgun rang out and echoed back and forth off of the mountains filling the valley with noise. He was a good 40 yards from me, but I jumped and ducked like a mortar round was coming in. Suddenly I was back in Korea clearing houses, then Southern was bleeding out in the back of the Humvee, then there was the Korean man plain as day lent up against a tree dead. I could smell the gun powder. When I came to I was still knelt on the ground and dad was yelling "Hey! Hey! Are you ok?" I stood up and said "yeah, I believe I am going to ride home. I gotta go." He said "I will load the dogs and take you." I said "no need it is just a mile or so back to the car. I will walk."

As I was walking along I started thinking "I could end it all right here right now with this shotgun." No then my dad would find me. That would haunt him forever and he would blame himself for letting me walk. Then he might feel like committing suicide. Wow! That would bother me. My father taking his own life was a scary thought. WOW! That is exactly how my kids would feel also. I gotta get help, if not for my family then for my friends. I need to call someone NOW!!

I called my SFC Booker when got back to the car. I said "I think I need help. I am drinking a 12 pack a day and everything gives me a flash back, and now Swann is gone I need some help. He said "ok and gave me the number to behavioral health Instead of being his usual tough self he actual seemed to care. He said "there ain't no shame in getting help. The shame is taking your life and ruining your families lives. I said "Roger SGT." then I hung up. I called behavioral health they arranged a meeting with me immediately. I got the help I needed and it saved my life. Thank God I was not one of the 22 Soldiers

Chapter 16: I'm still here

I thank God every day I got the help I needed. I called my brother on the way home, and I said "please pray for me I got the help I needed but every day will be a struggle." He said "God has a plan for you he don't make mistakes. He brought you through all of that to show you something, or to get you where he wants you. He works in mysterious ways so there is a reason you are still here, and you are right where he wants you to be." I told him "I love him very much." Then we hung up. I don't know where I would be without my brother, and Renee. They helped me more than anyone when I came home from the deployment.

I got home and walked in the house my little boy came running like always. Daddy! Daddy! Daddy! I grabbed him in my arms and just held him thinking "Thank you Lord for each and every blessing you have given me." I went on into the bedroom to find Renee sitting on the bed holding a piece of paper. I could tell she had been crying because her eyes were red and puffy. I asked "what's wrong?" She said "Nothing I am just so happy you came home to us and you are ok." I said "I am too. What are you reading?" She said "I went out to the shed to get the Christmas decorations out and I looked in your box from your deployment I was going to use some of your things for my scarp booking. On top of all of your stuff was this letter with my name on it." I said "yeah, I meant to throw that away when I got home. It is the letter for you if I died over there." She hugged me tight and said "I am just so happy you are here and alive. I said "don't be sad Honey I'm still here! The letter read:

Dear Renee,

If you are reading this then you know by now that I won't be coming home. I am afraid it wasn't meant to work out like we had planned. I am sorry I won't be there to walk Hadley down the aisle and give her away to her new husband and the love of her life. I won't be there to teach Emma how to drive a car, surprise her with her first car, or wait up with you worried sick when she isn't home on time. I won't be there to take Jay to his first day of school or watch him shoot his first Bear. I wish things would have been different. I wish I never had to come fight this war. I wish I would be there to run the grand children with you, or spoil them with Chocolate and toys just like our parents have done with our kids. I will be writing a separate letter for my brother and dad, but basically it will say: Please look after my Kids for me, and help Renee every chance you get.

I want you to know that you are the best thing that ever happened to me and you truly made my life worth living. I want to thank you for giving me the gift of being a father and a husband even if it was just for a few years. Each and every day spent with you and the kids was a true blessing. So please don't cry just be thankful for the many mornings we had together eating breakfast and preparing for our day, and our many nights lying there in the dark holding each other and talking about how our day was and our plans for tomorrow. Do me one favor and never forget that I loved you. I loved you and the kids more than anyone has ever loved anything. I have to go now it is time for me to load up for my first mission.

You're one True Love,
JS

Chapter 17: Long Road Ahead

It would be almost a year before I got over my "Shell Shock" as some call it. I am still a little jumpier than most from time to time. I just recently got to where I could watch a firework show without getting all tore up and have to leave. I still struggle with large crowds and where I sit in restaurants. I guess it is just something I have to live with. I been attending counseling at least once a month. I know some people may think it is a sign of weakness, but I am still here for my family. So I don't care what other say.

I have now served 10 years with one deployment to Iraq and one to Korea. I work full time active duty for the National Guard now. It is a great job with great benefits, so I can finally afford health insurance for my family. People have asked me "why do you still do it? Why do you keep re-enlisting? Aren't you scared of being deployed?" I give many different answers to these questions, but the real answer is. "I have been doing it so long I feel institutionalize I don't know how I would do anything else." As far as deploying "yes, I miss my family a lot when I am gone and yes the thought of going back is quite scary, but it is nowhere near as scary as the war coming here and my family being caught up in gun fire and Suicide bombers. You see we go over there to fight so people here in the states can go on living not having to worry about a bomb being dropped on their kid's school while they are at work, or someone kicking in their door and killing they're whole family in front of them because they refused to join the military. That is why this is the greatest country on earth and the land of the free.

Renee and I have talked about what happens if I get deployed again. I said "we both know it will happen all we can do is take away what we learned on the last deployment and try to do better on the next. The kids will be older next time, so that might make it easier". Renee Said "I don't think it ever gets easier I need you here I don't think I could go through all of the worrying again Mr." I constantly assure her it will be fine. I am planning on being a part of the military as long as they will have me.

Special Thanks:

There are many different methods to doing things in life. A lot of people like to do things their own way, and that is fine if it works. I talked with a fellow Soldier after he read this book and gave me some feedback. His only question was: How did you do it? I asked "How did I do what?" He said make it through all you of the stuff you went through over there and when you got home. Well the answer is really simple.

When I was in basic training like a lot of other Soldiers have done I asked myself is this where I need to be? Is this the life for me? During one of my toughest nights in basic training I was about 3 weeks in and I was tired, and really missing home. I bowed my head after lights out and prayed. I said "Lord if this is where you want me to be and what you want me to do, then make it to where I can do it. Make it possible for me to succeed. Amen"

Now every time I come to an obstacle or tough place in life. I say Lord help me trust in your plan and make this possible for me to do if you want me to do it. That is all I do. Also I have to give credit to all of my Army brothers and sister that have talked to me and helped me through a lot of things in my Life. Thank you SSG J!

Dedication

This book is dedicated to the people that made me who I am today.

Bobby Shelton (My Dad) - The man that raised me and taught me how to be a father and a husband.

Jason Shelton (My Brother) - The boy that became a man right by my side. That has always been there for me and just a phone call away no matter what.

Patricia Shelton (My Mom) - The woman that gave me life and my outgoing personality.

Made in the USA
Columbia, SC
09 April 2019